The Secrets of Gaining Wealth in Islam

Muddassir Khan

Published by Muddassir Khan, 2024.

Table of Contents

The Secrets of Gaining

Wealth in Islam

Muddassir Khan

While every precaution has been taken in the preparation of this book, the publisher assumes no responsibility for errors or omissions, or for damages resulting from the use of the information contained herein.

Introduction

Indeed, all praise is due to Allah. We praise Him, seek His help, and ask for His forgiveness. We seek refuge in Allah from the evils of ourselves and from our bad deeds. Whomsoever Allah guides, none can misguide him, and whomsoever He leads astray, none can guide him. I bear witness that there is no deity but Allah, alone, without any partners, and I bear witness that Muhammad is His servant and Messenger. May Allah's blessings and peace be upon him, his family, and his companions.

Narrated Rifaa bin Rafi: Allah's Messenger (peace and blessings of Allah be upon him) was asked what type of earning was best, and he replied: "A man's work with his hand and every approved business transaction."

"O you who have believed, fear Allah as He should be feared and do not die except as Muslims." "O mankind, fear your Lord, who created you from one soul and created from it its mate and dispersed from both of them many men and women. And fear Allah, through whom you ask one another, and the wombs. Indeed, Allah is ever, over you, an Observer." "O you who have believed, fear Allah and speak words of appropriate justice. He will [then] amend for you your deeds and forgive you your sins. And whoever obeys Allah and His Messenger has certainly attained a great attainment."

It is Allah who provides for us; therefore, we should seek our provision from Him. Allah says:

"We do not ask you for provision (i.e., to give Us something: money, etc.); We provide for you." [Surah Taa-Haa (20):132]

"And do not kill your children for fear of poverty. We provide for them and for you." [Surah Al-Isra (17):31]

The keys to sustenance mentioned in the Book of Allah and the Sunnah of His Messenger, peace be upon him, are numerous. They suffice the Muslim from seeking sustenance through sin. In this book many reasons that lead to sustenance are mentioned, and they are detailed with their clear evidences.

It has been authentically reported from the Prophet, peace and blessings be upon him, that he said: "If the son of Adam were to flee from his sustenance as he flees from death, his sustenance would still reach him just as death will reach him." This was narrated by Abu Nu'aym in "Hilyat al-Awliya" and graded as good by al-Albani.

This hadith indicates that a person will be provided with sustenance despite themselves, and if Allah, the Glorified and Exalted, has decreed sustenance for someone, it will not miss them and will not be lost to them as long as Allah has guaranteed it. Allah, the Exalted, has assured us of sustenance when He said: "And in the heaven is your provision and whatever you are promised." [Al-Dhariyat: 22]. Then He did not suffice with the assurance but also swore an oath to it, saying: "Then by the Lord of the heaven and the earth, it is indeed the truth, just as [it is true] that you can speak." [Al-Dhariyat: 23]. Al-Hasan al-Basri, may Allah have mercy on him, said: "May Allah curse people who were sworn to by their Lord and yet did not believe Him."

This book is a review of a blessed and beneficial message authored by Dr. Fadl Ilahi. This message is titled "The Keys to Sustenance in the Light of the Book and the Sunnah." In it, he has compiled many causes that are real reasons for attracting sustenance and blessing in it.

Allah, the Glorified and Exalted, has guaranteed sustenance and predestined it with the Pen of decrees. However, many Muslims occupy themselves with this guaranteed aspect at the expense of the non-guaranteed aspect. Sustenance is guaranteed, while salvation in the Hereafter and entering Paradise are not guaranteed, as they are dependent on the effort of the servant: "And that there is not for man except that [good] for which he strives." [An-Najm: 39]. We find it surprising that many people, when asked to stop pursuing the world which distracts them from obedience and worship, speak about sustenance and earning, and the necessity for a person to seek their provision, even though sustenance is guaranteed and salvation in the Hereafter is not guaranteed. Indeed, salvation depends on striving in righteous deeds.

Some people believe that adhering to their religion might decrease their sustenance. Even some of the devout who maintain Islamic obligations might think they must overlook some Islamic rulings to preserve financial prosperity. They forget or pretend to forget that when Allah, the Glorified and Exalted, legislated His religion, He aimed to guide the servants to their happiness in this world and the Hereafter, not just the Hereafter. Among the supplications of the Prophet, peace be upon him, was: "O Allah, give us good in this world and good in the Hereafter and protect us from the punishment of the Fire." Allah, the Glorified and Exalted, did not leave us groping in the dark and confused about seeking livelihood. Rather, the causes of sustenance were legislated and clarified. If the nation understood, grasped, adhered to them, and used them well, Allah, the Glorified and Exalted, would ease sustenance for them. Allah is the Provider, the Possessor of Strength, the Firm.

The issue of obtaining sustenance is a central concern for many people. In fact, a large number of people falsely believe that adhering to the teachings of the Quran and Sunnah results in a decrease in sustenance. What is more astonishing and saddening is that some seemingly religious people also hold the belief that it is necessary to overlook some of the Islamic teachings to achieve economic prosperity and well-being. These naive people are either unaware of this fact or have forgotten it despite being aware that the religion sent down by the Owner and Creator of the universe, Allah (May His Majesty be exalted), provides guidance not only for the Hereafter but also for worldly affairs. Just as the purpose of this religion is to elevate and honor humans in the Hereafter, Allah has also sent down this religion so that humanity, by adhering to it, may lead a life of happiness and prosperity in this world as well. The Messenger of Allah (peace and blessings be upon him), whom Allah, the Owner of the Kingdom, declared as a perfect example for all humanity, frequently asked for goodness in both this world and the Hereafter in his most invoked supplication.

Imam Bukhari has narrated from Hazrat Anas (may Allah be pleased with him) that he said:

The most frequent supplication of the Prophet (peace and blessings be upon him) was: "Our Lord, give us in this world [that which is] good and in the Hereafter [that which is] good and protect us from the punishment of the Fire." "The most frequent supplication of the Prophet (peace and blessings be upon him) was: 'Our Lord, give us in this world [that which is] good and in the Hereafter [that which is] good and protect us from the punishment of the Fire.'" (Al-Baqarah: 201).

In the matter of earning a livelihood, Allah Almighty and His noble Messenger (peace and blessings be upon him) have not left mankind groping in the dark. Rather, the means of obtaining sustenance have been thoroughly explained in the Book and the Sunnah. If humanity understands these means well, grasps them firmly, and utilizes them correctly, then Allah, the Owner of all sovereignty, who is the Sustainer and the Mighty, will open the doors of sustenance for people from all directions. He will send down blessings and bounties upon them from the sky and will cause various and abundant blessings to emerge for them from the earth.

"And in the heaven is your provision, and that which you are promised. Then, by the Lord of the heaven and the earth, it is the truth (i.e. what has been promised to you), just as it is the truth that you can speak." [Surah Adh-Dhaariyaat (51): 22-23]

It is our duty to strive for that which has been decreed for us.

The fact that it is Allah who provides for us does not negate the fact that we need to seek the means to reach what has been decreed for us. Just as it is decreed that we will feel hunger, no one would sit in one place without making an effort to satisfy the hunger and rely only on the fact that Allah will provide food. He will seek the means to alleviate the hunger.

Similarly, with our livelihood, we will never obtain what is not decreed for us, but we have to strive for what is decreed. Allah says:

"So, when the prayer is finished, spread out through the earth and seek Allah's bounty, and remember Allah often so that you may be successful." [Surah Al-Jumu'ah (62): 10]

The Messenger of Allah said: "If you were to truly trust in Allah, He would provide for you just as He provides for the birds which go out hungry in the morning and return full in the evening."

Now some of us might misunderstand this saying of the Prophet to mean that wherever we are, we will get our provision, but they should also note that the birds actually go out; they do not stay in their nests all day.

Allah Almighty has made His provision sufficient for every living being among His creations out of His grace and mercy. He has decreed the provision of man and written it while he is in his mother's womb, as reported by Muslim: "One of you is gathered in his mother's womb for forty days... then the angel is sent to breathe the soul into him, and he is commanded with four words: to write down his provision, his lifespan, his deeds, and whether he will be wretched or blessed..."

It is authentically reported from him, peace and blessings be upon him, in a hadith narrated by Abu Darda' that he said: "Provision seeks the servant just as his lifespan seeks him." This is found in the works of Ibn Abi Asim, Al-Daraj, Al-Bazzar, Ibn Hibban, Al-Tabarani in Al-Kabir, and Al-Bayhaqi, with this wording except that in Al-Tabarani it says: "more than his lifespan seeks him."

The Prophet, peace and blessings be upon him, said: "Allah has apportioned your morals among you just as He has apportioned your provisions among you..."

For a wisdom desired by Allah - the Almighty - He made this decree, and division of provisions hidden from the servants and concealed from them, {And no soul knows what it will earn tomorrow, and no soul knows in what land it will die.}.

Just as His will, the Almighty, desired that He made wealth beloved to souls and desired by nature and instinct, He said: {Wealth and children are [but] adornment of the worldly life...}, and He said: {And you love wealth with immense love.}.

There is no doubt that wealth contains good for a person if he uses it well in its rightful places, and Allah has called it good as He said: {Prescribed for you when death approaches [any] one of you if he leaves wealth [is that he makes] a bequest for the parents and near relatives according to what is acceptable - a duty upon the righteous.}.

And the Prophet (peace and blessings be upon him) said: "What an excellent wealth the lawful wealth is for a righteous man." Part of a long hadith by Amr ibn Al-As (may Allah be pleased with him) narrated by Ahmad, Al-Tabarani, and Abu Ya'la, this is the wording of Ahmad and Al-Tabarani, and in Abu Ya'la: "O Amr, excellent is the lawful wealth for a righteous man."

So wealth is good, it is beloved and righteous, necessary for fulfilling a person's needs in both his life and hereafter, as it is a means to perform many acts of worship such as pilgrimage and Umrah, zakat, charities, expiations, vows, maintaining family ties, seeking knowledge, and other benefits.

And even though provision is decreed by Allah the Almighty as mentioned earlier, He - the Exalted - decrees what He wills through causes that He has made mandatory for their effects; therefore, there is an encouragement and command to strive in seeking provision by taking the means to increase goodness and attain blessings in wealth so that life continues on the face of the earth, and a person refrains from asking others, avoiding the humiliation of need and poverty in his livelihood.

And to ensure that a person's striving in seeking provision is good, blessed, profitable, and praiseworthy, not a loss and detriment returned upon him, Islam has guided him to enter the houses of provision and attain blessings and growth through their doors, and to follow the means that bring about goodness and blessings and not others.

We should seek our earnings through prescribed means, and it is necessary to know which methods are not permissible. Only when we know that something is not permissible can we avoid it.

And since many people - for quite a long time - have let the love of wealth possess their hearts, and its desire has completely taken over their souls, as if they were created solely for that purpose, they have rolled up their sleeves, taking on difficult and easy tasks to acquire provisions and increase wealth, not content with seeking and striving by entering the houses of provision through their doors, but rather, they are breaking in through every window and opening with greed and voracity, not adhering to legitimate ways, nor caring about the reprehensible outcomes. They - or most of them - frequently complain about the lack of provision, the loss of blessings from salaries and wealth, and the lack of success in life's affairs and interests.

In this book, with the help of Allah Almighty, many means of sustenance are highlighted from the Quran and the Sunnah. Perhaps the Merciful Lord will provide guidance in it for those misguided Muslim brothers who are engrossed in their efforts to earn a livelihood but are either unaware of the legitimate means of obtaining sustenance or have forgotten them despite being aware, and are entangled in misconceptions about them.

So lets learn the keys that open the doors of wealth and sustenance.

Seeking Forgiveness and Repentance

One important means through which sustenance is sought from Allah is by seeking forgiveness and repenting to Him.

We will not speak about other material causes because the believer, the disbeliever, the righteous, and the wicked are equal in practicing them. Indeed, people's temptation, except for those whom Allah has mercy on, is in their preoccupation with seeking the worldly life to the extent that it distracts them from the Hereafter. We will not speak about natural causes because people do not need anyone to encourage them towards these causes, which are known to everyone and are taken care of by everyone. However, we will focus on the real spiritual and religious causes that most people are ignorant of and do not believe affect the pursuit of sustenance. Here, we will first establish the cause and then mention the evidence that it is a key to sustenance.

Whoever wants to attract lawful and blessed sustenance, the first thing to seek it with is repentance and seeking forgiveness from Allah, the Exalted. Seeking forgiveness and repentance are among the causes of sustenance. It is not meant that mere verbal repentance and seeking forgiveness, like the repentance of liars, is sufficient, but rather that repentance and seeking forgiveness must be from the heart, and their effect must then reflect on the limbs.

Al-Raghib al-Isfahani says: Repentance in Shariah means to abandon the sin for its ugliness, to regret what has been missed, to resolve not to repeat it, and to make amends for whatever is possible to rectify through repeated actions. When these four are combined, the obligations of repentance are complete.

Imam Al-Nawawi, may Allah have mercy on him, said: Scholars have said that repentance is obligatory from every sin. If the sin is between the servant and Allah and does not involve the right of another person, it has three conditions: First, to cease committing the sin and not persist in it, meaning that if the person does not abandon the sin, where is the repentance, and his state contradicts his claim? Second, to regret having done it. Third, to resolve never to return to it in the future. If one of these three conditions is missing, the repentance is not valid. If the sin involves the right of another person, a fourth condition is added: to absolve oneself of the right of the person. If it is money, it must be returned; if it is a grievance or similar, the person must be allowed to seek retribution or asked for forgiveness. If it is backbiting, one must seek forgiveness from the person.

Seeking forgiveness is asking for forgiveness through words and actions. Allah says: "So I said, 'Ask forgiveness of your Lord. Indeed, He is ever a Perpetual Forgiver.'" [Noah: 10]. They were not commanded to ask for it merely with the tongue but with both words and heart. It was said: Seeking forgiveness with the tongue without action is the act of liars. A liar's seeking forgiveness is to seek forgiveness with the tongue while persisting in disobedience to Allah, the Exalted.

There is much evidence that seeking forgiveness and repentance are among the causes that bring down Allah's sustenance, among them: Allah, the Exalted, says, narrating from Noah, peace be upon him, that he said to his people: "So I said, 'Ask forgiveness of your Lord. Indeed, He is ever a Perpetual Forgiver. He will send [rain from] the sky upon you in [continuing] showers and give you increase in wealth and children and provide for you gardens and provide for you rivers.'" [Noah: 10-12]. All these actions occur in response to the command: "Ask forgiveness of your Lord. Indeed, He is ever a Perpetual Forgiver." The meaning is: If you ask forgiveness from your Lord, He will send down rain upon you in abundance, and He will increase you in wealth and children and provide for you gardens and rivers.

First, seeking forgiveness must be realized. "Ask forgiveness of your Lord," meaning: Ask Him for pardon and forgiveness. "Indeed, He is ever a Perpetual Forgiver," so He will accept your repentance and forgive you. "He will send [rain from] the sky upon you in [continuing] showers," meaning He will send rain upon you continuously. "And give you increase in wealth and children," meaning He will increase your wealth and children. "And provide for you gardens and provide for you rivers," meaning gardens and rivers.

Al-Qurtubi, may Allah have mercy on him, says: In this verse and the verse in Hud, which says: "And O my people, ask forgiveness of your Lord and then repent to Him," [Hud: 52], there is evidence that seeking forgiveness brings down sustenance and rain.

Ibn Kathir, may Allah have mercy on him, says in his interpretation: If you repent to Allah, the Exalted, and seek His forgiveness and obey Him, He will increase your sustenance, shower you with the blessings of the heavens, and bring forth the blessings of the earth, He will grow crops for you, increase your livestock, grant you wealth and children, and make gardens for you with various fruits, interspersed with flowing rivers.

The Commander of the Faithful, Umar ibn Al-Khattab, may Allah be pleased with him, expressed this understanding when he prayed for rain with the people. Masrif narrated from Al-Sha'bi that Umar, may Allah be pleased with him, went out to pray for rain with the people and did not add anything more than seeking forgiveness until he returned. It was said to him: "We did not hear you ask for rain!" meaning: You did not say: "O Allah, give us rain," in the prayer for rain. Why did you limit yourself to seeking forgiveness?

Then Umar, may Allah be pleased with him, recited: "Ask forgiveness of your Lord. Indeed, He is ever a Perpetual Forgiver. He will send [rain from] the sky upon you in [continuing] showers" [Noah: 10-11] until the end of the verses.

Similarly, Al-Hasan Al-Basri, may Allah have mercy on him, advised every person who came to him complaining of drought, poverty, lack of offspring, or dryness of the orchard to seek forgiveness. Rabi' ibn Subaih said: A man complained to Al-Hasan about drought and dryness, and he told him: Seek forgiveness from Allah. Another complained to him about poverty, and he told him: Seek forgiveness from Allah. Another said to him: Pray to Allah to grant me a child. He told him: Seek forgiveness from Allah. Another complained to him about the dryness of his orchard, and he told him: Seek forgiveness from Allah. He said: We asked him about that, meaning: They asked him the reason behind his consistent advice to seek forgiveness despite the variety of needs. Rabi' ibn Subaih said to him: Men came to you complaining of various types of distress, and you advised them all to seek forgiveness. He said: I did not say anything from myself. Indeed, Allah, the Exalted, says in Surah Noah: "So I said, 'Ask forgiveness of your Lord. Indeed, He is ever a Perpetual Forgiver. He will send [rain from] the sky upon you in [continuing] showers and give you increase in wealth and children and provide for you gardens and provide for you rivers.'" [Noah: 10-12].

Verses like this include Allah's saying when He narrated Hud's call to his people: "And O my people, ask forgiveness of your Lord and then repent to Him. He will send [rain from] the sky upon you in showers and increase you in strength [added] to your strength. And do not turn away, [being] criminals." [Hud: 52]. He commanded them to seek forgiveness, which erases past sins, and to repent for what they will face. Whoever possesses these two qualities, Allah, the Exalted, will make their sustenance easy, facilitate their matters, and preserve their deeds.

Thus, He said: "He will send [rain from] the sky upon you in showers and increase you in strength [added] to your strength. And do not turn away, [being] criminals." [Hud: 52].

Also, His saying: "And [saying], 'Seek forgiveness of your Lord and repent to Him. He will let you enjoy a good provision for a specified term and give every doer of favor his favor. But if you turn away, then indeed, I fear for you the punishment of a great Day.'" [Hud: 3]. "He will let you enjoy a good provision" means: He will grant you abundant sustenance and a comfortable life and will not destroy you with punishment as He did to those who were destroyed before you. Allah has made this reward conditional on seeking forgiveness and repentance.

Among the evidence that seeking forgiveness and repentance are keys to sustenance is the hadith narrated by Imam Ahmad, Abu Dawud, Al-Nasa'i, Ibn Majah, and Al-Hakim from Abdullah ibn Abbas, may Allah be pleased with him, who said: The Messenger of Allah, peace and blessings be upon him, said: "Whoever frequently seeks forgiveness, Allah will make for him a way out of every worry, relief from every distress, and will provide for him from where he does not expect."

"Whoever frequently seeks forgiveness"

means: Whoever is prevalent in seeking forgiveness from Allah, the Exalted, upon committing a sin or when a calamity appears. Or: "Lazem (adheres to) seeking forgiveness" means: He persists in it because he needs it at all times. Hence, it is authentically reported that he, peace and blessings be upon him, said: "Blessed is the one who finds in his record a lot of seeking forgiveness" in the Hereafter. He did not say: Blessed is the one who frequently seeks forgiveness because it is a condition for seeking forgiveness to benefit a person that it be sincere. Only sincere seeking forgiveness, done with honesty and in harmony between words and actions, will be recorded. Therefore, he qualified it by saying it should be found in the record, not merely by seeking forgiveness. So his saying here: "Whoever frequently seeks forgiveness or adheres to seeking forgiveness, Allah will make for him a way out of every worry" means: He will make for him a way out of every distress that troubles him. "And relief from every distress" means: From every hardship and trial, a broad path will lead him to ease and comfort. "And will provide for him from where he does not expect" means: Lawful and good provision from sources he does not anticipate, hope for, or even imagine.

The discussion on this topic, by Allah's grace, is presented under two headings below:

1. The Reality of Seeking Forgiveness and Repentance

1. Four Evidences of Seeking Forgiveness and Repentance as a Cause of Sustenance

The Reality of Seeking Forgiveness and Repentance:

Many people think that seeking forgiveness and repentance is only related to verbal expression. There are many who verbally say:

"I seek forgiveness from Allah and repent to Him,"

but these words neither affect their hearts nor are reflected in their actions.

Two Scholars' Opinions:

1. Allama Raghib Isfahani writes:

"In Sharia, repentance means abandoning sin due to its abomination, feeling remorse for one's mistake,"

Resolve not to do it in the future, and to make an effort to the best of one's ability to compensate for the actions that can be rectified by performing them again. And when these four things are combined, the conditions of repentance are fulfilled."

Allama Raghib Isfahani writes about seeking forgiveness: "Seeking forgiveness (Istighfar) is asking for the forgiveness of sins through both speech and action. Allah Almighty's esteemed statement is: 'Seek forgiveness from your Lord; indeed, He is ever a Perpetual Forgiver.' In this directive, seeking forgiveness for sins is not only commanded through speech but through both speech and action. Asking for the forgiveness of sins merely with the tongue without action is the way of the greatest liars."

1. Imam Nawawi has written: "The scholars have said: Repentance from every sin is obligatory. If the sin is only between the servant and Allah Almighty, and it does not involve another person, then the following conditions are necessary for repentance from this sin: 1. Abandon the sin. 2. Feel remorse for it. 3. Resolve not to commit it again in the future."

If any one of these three conditions is missing, then his repentance is not valid. And if the sin involves another person, then there are four conditions for repentance from this sin: the previous three conditions and the fourth condition, which is to fulfill the rights of the wronged person. If the right is in the form of money, then this money must be returned. If he falsely accused someone with a punishment of slander, he must provide the opportunity for the wronged person to enforce the penalty or request pardon and forgiveness. And if he has backbitten someone, he must ask for their forgiveness."

B: Four proofs that seeking forgiveness and repentance is a cause of sustenance: Numerous noble verses and honorable hadiths indicate that seeking forgiveness and repentance is one of the causes of attaining sustenance. Below are four proofs with appropriate explanation and detail: A: Allah Almighty stated regarding Prophet Noah (peace be upon him) that he said to his people: "So I said, 'Ask forgiveness from your Lord; indeed, He is ever a Perpetual Forgiver. He will send rain to you in abundance. And give you increase in wealth and children and provide for you gardens and provide for you rivers.'" The benefits of seeking forgiveness mentioned in these verses: Among the fruits received from Allah Almighty due to seeking forgiveness are five as follows: The proof of this is: "Indeed, He is ever a Perpetual Forgiver." The proof of this is: "He will send rain to you in abundance." Abdullah bin Abbas (may Allah be pleased with him) stated: "'In abundance' means abundant rain." The proof of this is: "And give you increase in wealth and children." Ata stated in its interpretation: "He will increase your wealth and children."

The proof of this is:

"And He will make gardens for you."

The flowing of rivers:

The proof of this is:

"And He will cause rivers to flow for you."

Al-Qurtubi writes:

"This verse and the verse in Surah Hud are evidence that asking for forgiveness for sins is related to requesting sustenance and rain."

Hafiz Ibn Kathir writes:

"If you repent to Allah Almighty, ask forgiveness for your sins, and obey Him, He will grant you abundant sustenance, send down rain of mercy from the sky, make the earth produce goodness and blessings, grow crops from the earth, provide milk from animals, grant you wealth and children, give you gardens with various fruits, and make rivers flow between these gardens."

The incident of Umar Farooq (may Allah be pleased with him):

Amir al-Mu'minin Umar ibn al-Khattab (may Allah be pleased with him) acted upon what was mentioned in these noble verses to request rain from Allah Almighty. Al-Qurtubi has reported from Imam Sha'bi that Umar (may Allah be pleased with him) went out with people to ask for rain. He only asked Allah Almighty for forgiveness for sins and returned.

When it rained, he was asked: "We did not hear you asking for rain."

He said: "I asked Allah Almighty for rain through which rain is obtained."

Then read these verses from the Holy Quran:

"Seek forgiveness from your Lord; indeed, He is the Perpetual Forgiver. He will send down rain to you in abundance."

The incident of Hasan al-Basri:

Four people came to Hasan al-Basri. Each of them described their own difficulties, and he advised all of them to seek forgiveness for their sins from Allah Almighty.

Al-Qurtubi narrated from Ibn Sabi' that a person complained to Hasan al-Basri about a famine, so he said to him: "Seek forgiveness from Allah Almighty for your sins."

The second person complained about poverty and destitution, so he said to him: "Seek forgiveness from Allah Almighty for your sins."

The third person came and requested: "Pray to Allah Almighty to grant me a son."

He advised him in response: "Request forgiveness for your sins from Allah Almighty."

The fourth person complained about the drought in his garden, so he said to him: "Plead with Allah Almighty for forgiveness for your sins."

(Ibn Sabi' says) We said to him:

Another narration states that Rabi' ibn Sabi' said to him:

"You had four people come with separate complaints, and you gave them all the same instruction: 'Seek forgiveness from Allah Almighty for your sins.'"

Hasan al-Basri replied: "I did not tell them anything from myself; I only instructed them according to what the Compassionate and Generous Lord has mentioned. Indeed, Allah Almighty says in Surah Noah (peace be upon him):

{Seek forgiveness from your Lord, indeed He is the Most Forgiving. He will send down upon you abundant rain from the sky. And He will increase you in wealth and children and make for you gardens and make for you rivers.}

Allah is Great! The benefits and rewards of seeking forgiveness are so magnificent and abundant. O Generous Lord! Include us among those who seek forgiveness and grant us the blessings of forgiveness in both this world and the Hereafter. You are indeed the One who hears and accepts supplications. Ameen, O Lord of the worlds.

2: Allah Almighty mentioned the invitation of Prophet Hud (peace be upon him) to his people, saying that he said to his people:

{And O my people, seek forgiveness from your Lord and then repent to Him. He will send down upon you abundant rain from the sky and increase you in strength upon your strength. And do not turn away as criminals.}

(And O my people! Seek forgiveness from your Lord for your past sins, then repent to Him (refrain from future sins). He will send down upon you abundant rain from the sky and will increase your strength, and do not turn back as criminals.)

In the commentary of this, Hafiz Ibn Kathir writes:

"Then he (Prophet Hud, peace be upon him) commanded his people to seek forgiveness from Allah for their past sins, so that previous mistakes are erased; and he also instructed them to refrain from future sins. Whoever possesses the virtue of (seeking forgiveness and repenting), Allah makes it easy for him to obtain sustenance, facilitates his matters, and protects him. That is why it is said:

'He will send down upon you abundant rain from the sky.'"

O our Generous Lord! Bestow upon us the blessing of repentance and seeking forgiveness, and then make the acquisition of sustenance easy for us. Facilitate our matters and be our supporter and helper in all our tasks. You are indeed the One who hears and accepts prayers. Ameen, O Lord of Majesty and Honor.

3: Allah Almighty says:

"And (commanding you) to seek forgiveness from your Lord and then repent to Him, He will let you enjoy a good provision for a specified term and give every doer of favor his favor. But if you turn away, then indeed, I fear for you the punishment of a great Day."

In this noble verse, there is a promise from Allah Almighty to grant a good provision to those who seek forgiveness and repent. And by (good provision), as stated by Ibn Abbas (may Allah be pleased with them), it means that He will grant you wealth and abundance in sustenance.

In his commentary, Allama Qurtubi writes:

"This is the result of seeking forgiveness and repenting, that Allah will grant you ample sustenance and prosperity, and He will not destroy you with punishment as He did with those before you."

In this noble verse, the relationship between seeking forgiveness and repenting and the expansion of sustenance is like the relationship between a condition and its reward. Seeking forgiveness and repenting are mentioned as the (condition), and the expansion of sustenance as the (reward). It is known that when the (condition) is fulfilled, the (reward) is also necessitated. Similarly, whenever there is seeking forgiveness and repenting from the servant, the Merciful and Generous Lord will surely grant him ample sustenance and prosperity. The famous Quranic commentator Sheikh Muhammad Amin Shinqiti writes:

"This noble verse indicates that seeking forgiveness and repenting from sins are the cause of ample sustenance, wealth, and prosperity because Allah has mentioned seeking forgiveness and repenting as the (condition) and wealth and prosperity as the (reward)."

4: Imams Ahmad, Abu Dawood, Nasa'i, Ibn Majah, and Hakim have narrated from Abdullah bin Abbas (may Allah be pleased with them), who said: "The Messenger of Allah (peace be upon him) said: "Whoever frequently seeks forgiveness from Allah, Allah will make a way out for him from every worry, and a relief from every hardship, and He will provide for him from where he does not expect."

In this hadith, the Prophet Muhammad (peace be upon him) mentioned three benefits and rewards for those who frequently seek forgiveness for their sins, and one of these three is that the Provider, Allah, will grant them sustenance from places they never imagined. There can be no doubt about the truth and authenticity of this news, for the one who conveyed it is the most truthful among all of Allah's creation, and he conveys it not from himself but from the revelation of Allah.

O seekers of sustenance! Frequently seek forgiveness and repentance. Distance yourselves from your sins. Shed tears of remorse for past misdeeds and resolve that you will never approach those sins for the rest of your life. And be particularly mindful that seeking forgiveness and repentance should not be mere words. Without the remorse of the heart and efforts towards rectifying actions, verbal seeking of forgiveness and repentance is the habit of liars and deceivers, and what value can such seeking of forgiveness and repentance have in the sight of Allah?

Taqwa (Piety)

Fear of Allah, the Mighty and Majestic, is one of the causes by which the provision of Allah, Glorified and Exalted, is brought down. There are many definitions of fear of Allah given by scholars. Al-Raghib Al-Isfahani said: Fear of Allah is preserving oneself from what brings sin, by avoiding the prohibited, and this is completed by leaving some of the permissible.

Imam Al-Nawawi defined fear of Allah as: Complying with His commands and prohibitions, which is the protection from His wrath and punishment, by doing actions that are a shield and barrier between oneself and the fire.

Al-Jurjani defined it as: Guarding oneself by obeying Allah from His punishment, which is preserving oneself from what deserves punishment, whether by action or omission.

Whoever does not guard himself from what brings sin is not upright. Whoever sees with his eyes what Allah has forbidden, it means that he has removed the veil between him and the fire and deserves the punishment of Allah because he did not fear Allah and did not restrain his eyes from committing the sin that displeases Allah. Whoever commits the sin has removed this veil and plunged himself into the fire.

Likewise, whoever hears with his ears what displeases Allah, or uses his hands for what Allah does not approve of, or walks to what Allah despises, this person has not guarded himself from sin and has not feared Allah, Glorified and Exalted. Therefore, fear of Allah was the advice of Allah to the earlier and later people. Allah said: {And We have instructed those who were given the Scripture before you and yourselves to fear Allah} Even the prophets were commanded to fear Allah {O Prophet, fear Allah}.

As for the fact that fear of Allah is among the causes of provision, the evidence for this is His saying, Blessed and Exalted: {And whoever fears Allah - He will make for him a way out. And will provide for him from where he does not expect. And whoever relies upon Allah - then He is sufficient for him. Indeed, Allah will accomplish His purpose. Allah has already set for everything a [decreed] extent}.

We want to establish these concepts in our hearts. People who rush to the forbidden for fear of missing provision or engage in the forbidden for fear of lack of money do not know that the forbidden is not truly a cause of abundant provision, but rather it is a trial and tribulation.

{And whoever fears Allah - He will make for him a way out}, so whoever wants a way out should fear Allah, and thus he should stay away from prohibitions and doubtful matters. If he fears Allah, Glorified and Exalted, and is truthful in his fear, Allah has promised him a promise that He does not break, to make for him a way out and provide for him from where he does not expect. If he claims to fear Allah and has not found a way out, we say to him: Review yourself for you have not feared Allah as He should be feared. Return to yourself and correct your repentance; for Allah does not break His promise.

His saying, {He will make for him a way out}, means: He will save him from every distress in this world and the Hereafter. {And will provide for him from where he does not expect}, meaning: From where he does not hope or anticipate.

One of the evidences is His saying, Blessed and Exalted: {And if only the people of the cities had believed and feared Allah, We would have opened upon them blessings from the heaven and the earth; but they denied [the messengers], so We seized them for what they were earning} [The Heights: 96], meaning: If they had feared Allah, We would have expanded upon them goodness and made it easy for them from every direction.

Blessing (Barakah): It refers to growth, increase, and happiness. Ibn Manzur said something similar. Al-Zajaj said: "(Tabarak): a form derived from blessing, and the meaning of blessing: abundance in all things good." Ibn Kathir said: "Tabarak, derived from the blessing that is stable, permanent, and lasting."

Ibn Al-Athir said: The saying of the Prophet, "And bless Muhammad and the family of Muhammad," means to affirm and perpetuate what has been given to him of honor and dignity, which is from (Baraka al-ba'ir) if it kneels in a place and remains there. He said: Blessing also refers to increase and origin.

Blessings are the plural of blessing, and a blessing is the stability of divine goodness in something. The divine goodness that Allah, Glorified and Exalted, places in something remains in it, not disappearing or leaving it. From the word blessing, it is understood that Allah, Glorified and Exalted, gives them, because of faith and fear of Allah, continuous goodness that has no evil or consequence. The best of conditions is that the blessing Allah, Glorified and Exalted, provides to the servant remains, then He does not place a consequence upon it in the Hereafter and does not hold him accountable for it.

He, Blessed and Exalted, said: {We would have opened upon them blessings from the heaven and the earth} [The Heights: 96], and He did not say: A blessing, indicating the multiplicity of these blessings, considering the various types of blessed things. Blessings of the heaven with rain, blessings of the earth with plants and fruits, the abundance of livestock and cattle, and the attainment of security and safety; because the heaven serves as a father, and the earth serves as a mother, and from them all benefits and goodness for the creatures of Allah are obtained.

Al-Nawawi said regarding Allah's words: {So blessed be Allah, the best of creators}, it was said: it means goodness is established with Him, and it was said: exalted is He, and blessing is elevation and growth ... and its origin is from stability.

Al-Hafiz Ibn Hajar confirmed what Ibn Al-Athir and Al-Nawawi mentioned, saying regarding "and bless Muhammad": the intended meaning of blessing here is an increase in goodness and honor ... and it was said that it means affirming and continuing that, from the saying 'the camels knelt', meaning they remained on the ground, and hence the water pool is named so, because the water stays in it, and the essence is that the request is for them to be given the most goodness and for it to be established and continuous always.

From the above, it is clear that blessing is growth and increase in goodness, with the stability, establishment, and continuity of this goodness with its owner, and Allah knows best.

It is worth mentioning here that blessing does not necessarily always pertain only to abundance, but it can be in small things as well as in large things. This is what Al-Hafiz Ibn Hajar indicated in the hadith of Hakim ibn Hizam where he said: "And whoever takes it with greed, it will not be blessed for him, like the one who eats but is not satisfied ...".

Al-Hafiz said: in it is an analogy for what the listener does not comprehend of the examples, because the majority of people only recognize blessing in abundance, so the mentioned example was given to show that blessing is a creation of Allah, and an analogy was given with what they are familiar with.

It is also important to know that blessing can be apparent, or it can be hidden, and it may also be a reward in the hereafter. The apparent blessing is what is commonly seen with the increase of goodness and the provision of sustenance for a person, and its growth with its owner accompanied by success and ease in obtaining sustenance, and the like.

The hidden blessing may be in preventing harm, calamities, and afflictions from the sustenance, and in not exposing the person to accidents or severe diseases, and the like, which could take away a significant part of his sustenance. It was mentioned that if the livestock produces females, this is a hidden blessing because they grow and multiply, and if they produce males, this is hidden deprivation. And Allah knows best.

As for the hereafter blessing, it is the growth and multiplication of the reward in good deeds, which is clear and observed in many Quranic verses and prophetic traditions.

Sustenance: sustenance is what is beneficial like income and rain.

Ibn Manzur said: sustenance is known, and there are two types of sustenance: apparent for the bodies like food, and hidden for the hearts and souls like knowledge and sciences.

Al-Jurjani said: "Provision is a term for what God delivers to the animal to eat, and it includes both the lawful and unlawful."

But Al-Qurtubi said: "Provision, in reality, is what the living being is nourished with, and in it lies the sustenance of his spirit and the growth of his body. It is not permissible for provision to mean ownership, because animals are provided for, but they cannot be described as owners of their fodder."

He also said in another place - regarding God's words: {And spend out of what We have provided for them}: We have provided for them means we have given them, and provision means giving, and according to the people of the Sunnah, it is what is beneficial whether lawful or unlawful.

The provision referred to having blessings is the lawful provision, as it is impossible to imagine blessing occurring in unlawful provision. Although provision also includes apparent gifts and benefits and hidden gifts as mentioned, the focus here is on apparent provision, which means wealth. There is a general and specific relationship between provision and wealth; all wealth is provision, but not all provision is wealth. However, one term is often used in place of the other without issue.

Ibn Al-Athir said: "Wealth originally referred to what is owned of gold and silver, then it was extended to everything that is possessed and owned of tangible items. Among the Arabs, wealth mostly referred to camels, as they were their primary form of wealth. The term 'wealth' has been mentioned repeatedly in different contexts in the hadith, differentiated by context."

Abd Al-Salam Al-Abadi said: "Wealth is something that has material value among people and is lawfully permissible to benefit from in times of abundance and choice."

Among the verses that indicate that fear of Allah is among the causes of bringing down provision is His saying, Mighty and Majestic: {And if they had upheld the Torah, the Gospel, and what was revealed to them from their Lord, they would have consumed [provision] from above them and from beneath their feet. Among them are a moderate community, but many of them - evil is that which they do} [The Table Spread: 66], Allah informs about the people of the Book that if they had acted upon the Torah and the Gospel, and also acted upon the Quran; Allah, Glorified and Exalted, would have increased the provision descending upon them from the heaven and growing for them from the earth, and would have bestowed upon them the blessings of this world abundantly.

Allah, Glorified and Exalted, said: {And if they had remained on the right way, We would have given them abundant water to drink} [The Jinn: 16], meaning: If they had remained on the way that pleases Allah, He would have rewarded them for that by giving them abundant water to drink.

Fear of God Almighty and Drawing Near to Him through Acts of Obedience

God Almighty has commanded His servants to fear Him as He should be feared. He said: {O you who have believed, fear Allah as He should be feared and do not die except as Muslims}. Then He clarified in another verse that fear of Him should be according to one's capability and human ability: {So fear Allah as much as you are able and listen and obey}.

Moreover, He - Almighty and Exalted - has promised that whoever fears Him, obeying what He commands and avoiding what He forbids, will be saved from every distress that constricts people. He will also provide for them from unexpected sources, satisfy them with what He gives, and bless their provision. This is reflected in His words: {And whoever fears Allah - He will make for him a way out. And will provide for him from where he does not expect}.

Ibn Abbas - may God be pleased with them both - reported that the Prophet, peace and blessings be upon him, said: "No man leaves something for the sake of God, even though he is capable of it, except that God will give him what is better than that in this world before the Hereafter."

In several places with different chains of narration from Ahmad from Abu Qatada and Abu Al-Dahma - may God be pleased with them both

- who said: We came upon a man from the Bedouins who said: The Messenger of God, peace and blessings be upon him, took my hand and taught me from what God had taught him and said: "You will never leave something out of fear of God Almighty except that God will give you something better than it."

Among the examples is the story of Joseph - peace be upon him - with the wife of Al-Aziz, his refusal to commit a sin despite all means of safety being available to him, out of fear of God Almighty. Also, the story of the three men who took refuge in a cave and it collapsed on them. Each of them prayed to God with a righteous deed he had done. One of them loved his cousin dearly and repeatedly tried to seduce her, but she always refused. Eventually, she was forced by need to agree, and when he sat between her legs, she said: Fear God. He left her, though she was the most beloved person to him, out of fear of God. It is evident what happened to Joseph - peace be upon him - in this world and the Hereafter of blessings, honor, and empowerment. Similarly, what happened to the man who refrained from sin despite having the ability to commit it out of fear of God, was relief in this world, the lifting of distress from him and his companions, who also had righteous deeds. God knows best.

As it came in the narration of Muslim from the hadith of Anas ibn Malik - may God be pleased with him - raising it: "Indeed, if a disbeliever does a good deed, he is given his due in this world, but as for the believer, God stores up his good deeds for him in the Hereafter and provides for him in this world due to his obedience".

And He said: {If only they had upheld the Torah, the Gospel, and what was revealed to them from their Lord, they would have consumed provision from above them and from beneath their feet}.

And He said: {And if the people of the cities had believed and feared Allah, We would have opened upon them blessings from the heaven and the earth; but they denied [the messengers], so We seized them for what they were earning}. And He also said: {And if they had remained on the right path, We would have given them abundant water to drink}.

In these noble verses, there is an indication that fearing God - Almighty and Exalted - and following everything that came through the tongues of the prophets and messengers by performing the commands and avoiding the prohibitions, including the command to the People of the Book to follow what the Prophet, peace and blessings be upon him, brought because their books command that, all of this is a cause for the descent of the blessings from the sky in the form of abundant rain, the emergence of the blessings of the earth, the abundance of provision, and continuous eating from it with the presence of blessings in it.

Al-Qurtubi said: "And similar to this is {And whoever fears Allah - He will make for him a way out. And will provide for him from where he does not expect}.

So, fear of Allah is among the causes of provision as in these verses. Whoever thanks Allah for His blessing by obeying Him, Allah has promised him an increase, as Allah said: {And [remember] when your Lord proclaimed, 'If you are grateful, I will surely increase you [in favor]'} [Abraham: 7].

Whoever desires abundant provision and a comfortable life, let him guard himself from what brings sin, comply with the commands of Allah, and avoid His prohibitions.

So, one of the important causes of sustenance is fear of Allah (taqwa). Discussion regarding this is under the following two headings: a: Definition of Taqwa b: Two reasons why Taqwa is a cause of sustenance

a: Definition of Taqwa: Sayings of three scholars: The scholars of the Ummah have clearly explained the meaning of taqwa. Below are the sayings of three of them: 1: Allama Raghib Asfahani has defined taqwa in these words: "Protecting the self from what causes sin, and that is by leaving forbidden matters. And it is completed by leaving some permissible matters as well." 2: Imam Nawawi writes: "Following His commands and prohibitions, and its meaning: protection from His displeasure and punishment, Glorified and Exalted be He."

"Adhering to Allah's commands and prohibitions. And the meaning of Taqwa is that a person avoids actions that cause Allah's displeasure and punishment."

3: Allama Jurjani has written:

"Protecting oneself through obedience to Allah from His punishment, and it is safeguarding the self from what deserves punishment whether by action or omission."

"Whoever pollutes their soul with sins is not pious. Whoever looks at forbidden things with their eyes, listens to disliked things with their ears, touches forbidden things with their hands, or goes to places of Allah's displeasure, has not protected their soul from sin.

What relation do those who anger Allah by defiling themselves with sins and inviting His punishment have with the pious?

How can those who disregard Allah's commands and prohibitions be counted among the pious?"

B: Two reasons why piety is a cause of provision: Many noble verses indicate that piety is a cause of provision. Two of these verses, along with appropriate interpretation, are listed below: 1: Allah, the Lord of Glory, says: (And whoever fears Allah, He will make for him a way out and provide for him from where he does not expect.) In this blessed instruction, Allah, the Lord of Glory, has stated that a person who possesses the quality of piety will be granted two blessings by Allah: The first blessing is that Allah will grant him relief from every grief and trouble. Abdullah bin Abbas, may Allah be pleased with him, explains in the interpretation of "He will make for him a way out": "Allah will grant him relief from every grief in this world and the Hereafter." Rabee bin Khuthaim has explained: "Allah will create a way out for him from every situation that causes difficulty and trouble for people." The second blessing is that Allah will provide for him from where he does not expect. Hafiz Ibn Kathir writes in the interpretation of the aforementioned two verses: "Whoever becomes pious by complying with Allah's commands and refraining from what He has forbidden, Allah will create a way out for him from every difficulty and will provide for him from where he does not expect." Allah is Great! How immense and valuable are the blessings and benefits of piety! Abdullah bin Masood, may Allah be pleased with him, says: "The greatest verse in the Quran that provides relief from grief and distress is: 'And whoever fears Allah, He will make for him a way out.'" Allah, the Exalted, says: (And if only the people of the cities had believed and feared Allah, We would have opened upon them blessings from the heaven and the earth; but they denied [the messengers], so We seized them for what they were earning.)

(And if the people of the towns had believed and feared (avoided bad deeds, disbelief, and polytheism), We would certainly have opened up to them blessings from the heavens and the earth, but they denied, so We seized them for what they used to earn.)

In this noble verse, Allah has stated that if the people of the towns adopt two things: faith and piety, He will open the doors of blessings for them from every direction. Abdullah bin Abbas, may Allah be pleased with him, explains in the interpretation of "We would certainly have opened up to them blessings from the heavens and the earth":

"We would have made good abundant for them and facilitated its acquisition from every direction."

There are many points hidden in the promise of opening blessings from the heavens and the earth for those who have faith and piety. Here are three of them:

The word "blessings" is the plural of "blessing," and while interpreting "blessing," Imam Baghawi writes:

"Consistency and permanence on something."

And Allama Khazin writes in his interpretation:

"Continuity and permanence on a thing."

"Presence of divine goodness in something."

This implies that the benefit and advantage gained in return for faith and piety are not temporary or momentary, nor are they something that can be replaced by evil, but rather they are lasting and eternal good.

Syed Muhammad Rashid Rida describes the excellence and goodness of the blessings bestowed on those who have faith and piety as follows:

"The blessings and bounties bestowed upon the believers make them happy and content, and they give thanks to Allah. They use these blessings in ways that are good and avoid using them in places of evil and corruption. Because of this behavior upon receiving blessings and bounties, Allah increases His favors upon them and grants them the best reward in the Hereafter."

Sheikh Ibn Ashur, in his interpretation of "blessing," writes:

"It is the good that is free from any blame in the Hereafter, and this is the best state of blessing."

Sheikh Ibn Ashur explains the wisdom behind using the plural form:

"The purpose of using the plural form is to indicate the various types of blessed things that the people of faith and piety receive."

"Blessings from the heavens and the earth"

In explaining this divine command, Alama Razi writes:

"The blessings of the heavens come in the form of rain, and the blessings of the earth come in the form of plants, fruits, abundance of livestock, and the attainment of security and safety. The wisdom behind mentioning the blessings of the heavens and the earth is that the heavens are like a father and the earth is like a mother, and through both, all benefits and good things are provided by Allah's creation and management."

Therefore, anyone who seeks the expansion and abundance of sustenance should keep themselves away from all sins. They should fulfill the commands given by Allah, avoid the things He has forbidden, and keep themselves away from anything that could cause Allah's displeasure and the descent of His punishment, whether it be neglecting good deeds or committing evil.

Trust in Allah

A mong the causes of provision is reliance on Allah, Glorified and Exalted.

Al-Ghazali said: Reliance is the heart's dependence on Allah, Glorified and Exalted, to whom the believer entrusts his affairs.

Al-Manawi said: Reliance is showing helplessness and depending on the one relied upon.

So, you show helplessness and weakness to Allah, Glorified and Exalted, and depend on Him alone, Mighty and Majestic, believing that there is no actor in existence except Allah, Glorified and Exalted, and that everything existing in terms of creation, provision, giving and withholding, benefit and harm, poverty and wealth, sickness and health, death and life, and everything that is called existence is from Allah, Glorified and Exalted.

Among the evidence that reliance is one of the causes of bringing down provision is what Umar ibn Al-Khattab, may Allah be pleased with him, narrated: The Messenger of Allah, peace and blessings be upon him, said: (If you were to rely on Allah as He should be relied on, He would provide for you as He provides for the birds: they go out hungry in the morning and return full in the evening).

(They go out): They go at the beginning of the day.

(Hungry): The plural of hungry, meaning starving.

(And return): They return at the end of the day with their crops full
(Full): The plural of full-bellied, meaning satiated. In between, they

strive, and Allah, Glorified and Exalted, is the one who takes care of their provision.

In this hadith, the truthful and trustworthy, peace and blessings be upon him, explains that whoever relies on Allah as he should be relied upon is provided for just as the birds are provided for; because he relies on the Ever-Living who does not die, and whoever relies on Allah, He is sufficient for him, as He, Glorified and Exalted, said: {And whoever relies upon Allah, then He is sufficient for him}, meaning: He is enough for him. If you rely and depend on Allah alone, He will suffice you, and you will not need any other agent, as He, Mighty and Majestic, takes care of all your affairs, {And whoever relies upon Allah, then He is sufficient for him. Indeed, Allah will accomplish His purpose. Allah has already set for everything a [decreed] extent}.

It is established and known that reliance on Allah, Glorified and Exalted, does not necessitate abandoning earning, as those ignorant of the reality of reliance might believe, and some may use this hadith as evidence. The hadith itself refutes them because the Prophet, peace and blessings be upon him, when he gave us this example, we should take all its aspects. His saying: (They go out hungry and return full), indicates that they go out and return, meaning they move and strive while relying on Allah, Glorified and Exalted. Similarly, a person should strive for provision out of respect for the law because the law commands taking means, but one should not depend on the means but on the Creator of the means, who is Allah, Glorified and Exalted, as He is the true provider.

We take the means because Allah commanded us to take the means.

Scholars said: Abandoning the means is a flaw in the law, and depending on the means is a flaw in monotheism.

We take the means but do not attach our hearts to the means because they are created. Rather, our hearts should be attached to Allah, Mighty and Majestic. The birds go out and return, strive, and rely on Allah, Glorified and Exalted, and Allah takes care of their affairs, even though they do not understand or comprehend or plan or understand or manage. Allah, Glorified and Exalted, is the one who provides for them.

Imam Ahmad said: There is nothing in the hadith that indicates abandoning earning; rather, it indicates seeking provision. He meant that if they relied on Allah in their going out and coming back and their actions and knew that the good is in His hands, they would go out only successful and safe like the birds.

Imam Ahmad was asked about a man who sat in his house or the mosque and said: I will not do anything until my provision comes to me! He said: This man is ignorant of knowledge, for the Prophet, peace and blessings be upon him, said: (Allah made my provision under the shade of my spear).

Taking means is well-known and well-established in the law, and there are many examples of it in the Quran, including: {And shake toward you the trunk of the palm tree} [Mary: 25], it could have been that as soon as she raised her head, the fresh dates would fall by Allah's power, but this is an indication of the necessity of taking the means while relying on the Creator of the means, who is Allah, Glorified and Exalted.

Allah said about Moses: {So he left it, fearful and vigilant}, so Moses, peace be upon him, took the means to escape from Pharaoh, for when he knew they were plotting to kill him, he left it fearful and vigilant.

The Prophet, peace and blessings be upon him, also took the means during the migration journey, and these are well-known situations that we do not need to mention.

The companions, may Allah be pleased with them, used to trade and work in their palm groves.

Imam Abu Hamid said: It might be thought that reliance means abandoning earning with the body and abandoning planning with the heart and falling to the ground like a thrown rag or like meat on a chopping block. This is the thought of the ignorant, as this is forbidden in the law, and the law has praised the reliant. How can a rank of the religion be attained through something forbidden in the religion?! He means that reliance is praised in the law, and abandoning the means is forbidden in the law. Those who abandon the means and claim that it is reliance are sinful, and can a praised rank in religion be reached by a forbidden means?! The means to the obligatory or recommended must be lawful, and the means and causes take the ruling of the objectives. We do not have the principle: the end justifies the means. Rather, the means must be lawful and the end must be lawful as well.

Al-Qushayri said: Know that reliance is in the heart, and outward movement does not contradict reliance in the heart because reliance is a heart worship like repentance, sincerity, turning to Allah, and certainty.

All these acts of worship are performed by the heart, so reliance is a heart worship, and outward movement does not contradict reliance in the heart after the servant believes that provision is from Allah, Exalted is He, and if something is hindered, it is by His decree, and if something is facilitated, it is by His facilitation. A man said to the Prophet, peace and blessings be upon him: (Should I tie it and rely on Allah or leave it untied and rely on Allah? He said to him: Tie it and rely on Allah), as for leaving the camel untied without a rope or halter and saying: I rely on Allah, this is not reliance. Likewise, one should not leave his goods at the mosque door and say: I rely on Allah! Especially when there are many dishonest people who betray the worshippers during prayer and steal from them, will the mosque intercede for you if you act foolishly and neglect the means? No, tie it and rely on Allah, do not leave it to thieves on the road and then say: I rely on Allah, take the means and rely.

Some may leave the car open and then something is stolen from it, this person did not tie the camel, but left it open, he should have taken the means and not relied on them, and this is reliance on Allah, Glorified and Exalted.

In a narration by Imam Al-Qudai, Amr ibn Umayyah, may Allah be pleased with him, said: (I said: O Messenger of Allah! Should I tie my ride and rely on Allah or let it go and rely? He said: Tie it and rely).

So, reliance does not imply abandoning earning, rather a person should work hard and strive and seek livelihood, but he does not depend on his hard work, striving, and efforts, but believes that the matter is entirely in Allah's hands, and that provision is from Allah, Glorified and Exalted, alone.

So among the means through which sustenance is obtained, one significant cause is having trust (tawakkul) in Allah, the Owner of the Kingdom. The following three topics will be discussed regarding this subject:

a. The concept of trusting in Allah

b. Evidence of trust being the key to sustenance

c. Does trust mean abandoning efforts to obtain sustenance?

a. The concept of trusting in Allah:

Three scholars' opinions:

Scholars of the Ummah have clarified the meaning of trust.

1. **Al-Ghazali writes:**

   "Trust is the reliance of the heart solely on the one in whom trust is claimed."

1. **Al-Manawi writes:**

   "Trust is the demonstration of one's inability and reliance on the one who is trusted."

Trust in Allah

a. The concept of trusting in Allah:

"Trust is the expression of a servant's helplessness and complete reliance on the one in whom trust is placed."

3. Mulla Ali Qari, in his commentary on "Trust in Allah as it ought to be" writes:

"Know for certain that, in reality, all actions are performed by Allah. Everything in the universe—creation, sustenance, giving or withholding, harm and benefit, poverty and wealth, illness and health, death and life—everything is solely by Allah's command."

b. Evidence of trust being the key to sustenance:

Imams Ahmad, Tirmidhi, Ibn Majah, Ibn Mubarak, Ibn Hibban, Hakim, Qudai, and Bagawi have narrated from Abdullah bin Umar that the Prophet Muhammad (peace be upon him) said:

"If you were to trust in Allah as He should be trusted, you would be provided for as the birds are provided for: they go out hungry in the morning and return full in the evening."

"If you had relied on Allah as He deserves to be relied upon, you would have been provided for in the same way that birds are provided for: they leave in the morning empty and return in the evening full."

In this Hadith, the Prophet (peace be upon him) has informed the Ummah that those who truly rely on Allah are provided for in the same way that birds are provided for. And why wouldn't they be? The one who trusts in Allah relies on the Great, Unique, and Sovereign of the universe, who says "Be" and it becomes.

"Indeed, His command, when He intends a thing, is only that He says to it, 'Be,' and it is."

The one who trusts in Him alone is sufficient for them. Allah Himself has stated:

"And whoever relies upon Allah - then He is sufficient for him. Indeed, Allah will accomplish His purpose. Allah has already set for everything a decree."

In the interpretation of this, Rabi' bin Khuthaym states:

"Allah is sufficient for him against everything that causes hardship for people."

C: Does reliance on Allah mean abandoning the effort to obtain sustenance?

Some naive people might argue that if those who rely on Allah are indeed provided for, then why should we make efforts and work hard to earn our sustenance? Why not sit back and relax, expecting that sustenance will come down from the heavens due to reliance?

Such statements reflect ignorance about the concept of reliance. If these individuals reflected on the Hadith mentioned above, they would not make such claims. The Prophet (peace be upon him) compared those who rely on Allah to birds, which leave in the morning in search of sustenance and return in the evening satisfied with the grace of Allah. Despite the fact that these birds have no shops, factories, jobs, or fields where they put their trust for sustenance, their complete reliance for obtaining sustenance is solely on Allah.

The scholars of the Ummah have clarified this matter well. For instance, Imam Ahmad wrote: "The Hadith does not state that effort should be abandoned in the quest for sustenance. Instead, it indicates that one should strive to obtain sustenance. The Prophet (peace be upon him) meant that if one's efforts and striving are accompanied by the conviction that all goodness is in the hands of Allah, then they will certainly return with the blessings and sustenance as the birds return in the evening with their stomachs full."

When Imam Ahmad was asked about a person who sits at home or in the mosque and says: "I will not do any work; my sustenance will come to me on its own," he replied: "This person is ignorant." The Prophet (peace be upon him) said:

"Indeed, Allah has placed my sustenance under the shade of my spear."

And the Prophet (peace be upon him) also said:

"If you had relied on Allah as He deserves to be relied upon, He would have provided for you in the same way He provides for the birds: they leave in the morning empty and return in the evening full."

The Prophet (peace be upon him) indicated that birds leave in search of sustenance and return having found it.

The Imam also said: "The Companions (may Allah be pleased with them) engaged in trade and worked in their orchards (date palms). They are an example for us."

Shaykh Abu Hamid (Imam Al-Ghazali) writes:

"It is a foolish notion to think that reliance means abandoning physical effort and mental contemplation for obtaining sustenance, and simply lying on the ground like worn-out rags or resting on a board like a piece of meat. Indeed, such actions are prohibited in Sharia. Reliance is praised in Islam, and it is inconceivable that those who commit prohibited actions can be deemed praiseworthy by Sharia.

To clarify the truth, we say: The effect of reliance is evident in the efforts and endeavors made by an individual to achieve their goals."

Imam Abu Qasim al-Qushayri explains:

"The place of reliance is the heart. When an individual's heart firmly believes that sustenance comes from Allah, and if hardship occurs, it is due to divine decree, and if ease comes, it is due to His grace and generosity. After attaining this state, outward actions do not contradict reliance."

The following Hadith also indicates that reliance does not mean abandoning efforts to obtain sustenance:

Imam Ibn Hibban and Imam Hakim have narrated from Hadhrat Amr bin Umayya (may Allah be pleased with him) who said:

"A person said to the Prophet (peace be upon him):

'I will release my camel and rely on Allah.'

The Prophet (peace be upon him) replied:

'Tie it and then rely on Allah.'"

The Prophet (peace be upon him) said:

"Tie its knee and then rely on Allah."

In a narration by Imam Qazai, it is reported that Amr bin Umayya (may Allah be pleased with him) asked:

"O Messenger of Allah! Should I tie my mount and rely on Allah, or should I release it and rely on Allah?"

The Prophet (peace be upon him) replied:

"Tie it and rely on Allah."

In summary, reliance (Tawakkul) does not mean abandoning the effort to earn sustenance. It is the responsibility of a Muslim to strive for sustenance, but their trust should not be in their own effort and labor, but rather in the Lord of Glory. They should believe that all matters are in His hands and that sustenance comes only from Him.

Being Free for the Worship of Allah, the Mighty and Exalted

Among the causes of provision is devoting oneself to the obedience of Allah, Glorified and Exalted: The purpose of devoting oneself to the obedience of Allah, Mighty and Majestic, is not to abandon seeking livelihood and stay in the mosque day and night, but to keep one's heart always connected to Allah, Glorified and Exalted, in all circumstances without interruption. A believer does not keep an hour for his Lord, an hour for his devil, and an hour for his (spiritually) sick heart; as is the case with some people, where they pray in the mosque and then commit sins and forbidden acts outside the mosque, saying: an hour for your heart and an hour for your Lord, {That, then, is an unjust division} because the heart of a believer is connected to Allah, Mighty and Majestic, in all his circumstances, never breaking this connection. Some of the righteous predecessors were asked: Does the heart prostrate? He said: It prostrates a prostration from which it never raises its head, meaning: If it repents and returns to Allah, it remains in submission to Allah, Glorified and Exalted, and does not deviate from the state of prostration, remaining always prostrate. The heart of a believer, in all his circumstances, is connected to Allah, Mighty and Majestic, even while engaging in permissible entertainment or working in the world.

The meaning of devoting oneself to the obedience of Allah, Glorified and Exalted: is to worship Allah as if you see Him, and if you do not see Him, then He, Glorified and Exalted, sees you.

The evidence that devoting oneself to the worship of Allah, Mighty and Majestic, is one of the keys to provision is what Abu Huraira, may Allah be pleased with him, narrated from the Prophet, peace and blessings be upon him, who said: (Allah, Exalted, says: O son of Adam! Devote yourself to My worship, I will fill your chest with wealth and alleviate your poverty, but if you do not, I will fill your hands with work and not relieve your poverty).

(O son of Adam, devote yourself to My worship) means: strive to empty your heart for My worship.

(I will fill your chest with wealth) means: I will fill your heart, which is in your chest, with wealth; because true wealth is the wealth of the soul as the Prophet, peace and blessings be upon him, explained. This is the highest degree of wealth.

The poet says: I became rich without money, above all people, and true wealth is being free of need from anything, not the wealth you possess in your hands from the worldly goods, but the wealth of the soul and the wealth of the heart.

And His saying: (And alleviate your poverty) means: I will close the door of your need for people, (but if you do not, I will fill your hands with work and not relieve your poverty) He mentioned the hands because a person usually engages in earning with the hands, and most actions are done with the hands.

It is authentically reported from the Prophet, peace and blessings be upon him, that he said: (Whoever makes the world his concern, Allah will place poverty between his eyes, disorganize his affairs, and he will not get from the world except what is decreed for him. And whoever makes the Hereafter his concern, Allah will organize his affairs, place wealth in his heart, and the world will come to him, humbled).

And from Ma'qal ibn Yasar, may Allah be pleased with him, from the Prophet, peace and blessings be upon him, who said: (Your Lord, Blessed and Exalted, says: O son of Adam! Devote yourself to My worship, I will fill your heart with wealth and fill your hands with provision. O son of Adam! Do not distance yourself from Me, lest I fill your heart with poverty and fill your hands with work).

So, one of the means of provision is a person's being free for the worship of Allah, the Almighty. With divine guidance, the following two topics will be discussed on this matter:

A: The Concept of Being Free for the Worship of Allah

B: Two Evidence for Provision Resulting from Being Free for the Worship of Allah

A: The Concept of Being Free for the Worship of Allah:

This does not mean that a person should sit in the mosque day and night and make no effort for earning a livelihood; rather, it means that when a person worships Allah, both his heart and body should be present. There should be humility and reverence in worship. The greatness and majesty of the Lord of Glory should be embedded in his heart. He should have the awareness and realization that he is conversing with the Master of the universe, Allah. He should be the practical embodiment of the noble saying of the Prophet Muhammad (peace be upon him):

"Worship Allah as if you see Him."

If he cannot attain this state, then at least he should have:

"If you cannot see Him, then indeed He sees you."

"If you do not see Him, then indeed He sees you."

Do not be among those whose bodies are in the mosques, but their hearts are preoccupied and attached to external matters. Mulla Ali Qari writes in the explanation of the noble saying of the Prophet Muhammad (peace be upon him) (Tafarragh li'ibadatī):

"Exert effort in freeing your heart for the worship of your Lord."

B: Two Evidence for Provision Resulting from Being Free for the Worship of Allah:

1: The scholars, Ahmad, Tirmidhi, Ibn Majah, Ibn Hibban, and Hakim narrate from Abu Huraira (may Allah be pleased with him) from the Prophet Muhammad (peace be upon him), (that) the Prophet Muhammad (peace be upon him) said:

"Indeed, Allah, the Exalted, says:

"O son of Adam! Free yourself for my worship, I will fill your chest with wealth and make you independent of people.

And if you do not do so, I will fill your hands with (useless) work and will not end your poverty towards people."

In this hadith, the Prophet (peace be upon him) informed the Ummah that for those who worship Allah with full attention and focus, two rewards are promised by Allah:

First reward: Filling the heart with wealth.

Second reward: Making them independent of people.

In the same hadith, there is also a warning of two punishments from Allah for those who do not worship with attention and focus:

First punishment: Engaging them in useless work.

Second punishment: Not ending their dependency on people and always keeping them in need of others.

2: Imam Hakim narrated from Ma'qil bin Yasar (may Allah be pleased with him), that he said: "The Messenger of Allah (peace be upon him) said:

"Your Lord, blessed and exalted, says:

"O son of Adam! Free yourself for my worship, I will fill your heart with wealth and your hands with sustenance. O son of Adam! Do not distance yourself from me, for (if you do so) I will fill your heart with poverty and your hands with occupation."

Your Lord, blessed and exalted, says:

"O son of Adam! Free yourself for my worship, I will fill your heart with self-sufficiency and your hands with sustenance.

O son of Adam! Do not distance yourself from me (if you do so), I will fill your heart with poverty and your hands with (useless) work."

In this hadith, the Prophet (peace be upon him) informed the Ummah that for those who worship with complete attention and dedication, Allah the Almighty Himself has promised the following two rewards:

1: Filling their heart with richness.

2: Filling their hands with sustenance.

And it is known that Allah does not break promises.

(Indeed, Allah does not fail in His promise.)

In this hadith, the Prophet (peace be upon him) also informed the Ummah that for those who distance themselves from Allah, He has warned of the following two punishments:

1: Filling their heart with poverty.

2: Engaging them in useless tasks.

When the Creator of hearts and the Owner of treasures fills a heart with wealth, how can the feeling of neediness and the concept of dependency even come near it?

How can one, whose hands are filled with sustenance by the Provider of all creations, fall into poverty and destitution? If the solitary and unique Owner of the universe, Allah the Almighty, fills someone's heart with neediness, then even if all other forces unite and agree, they cannot make him rich and well-off. And if the Mighty and Compelling Allah entangles someone in useless and meaningless matters, who can possibly provide him with relief?

Consistency in Hajj and Umrah

Among the causes of provision is the alternation between pilgrimage and minor pilgrimage: The meaning of alternation is to make one follow the other consecutively, that is, if you perform the pilgrimage, then perform the minor pilgrimage, and if you perform the minor pilgrimage, then perform the pilgrimage. This is the meaning of alternation between pilgrimage and minor pilgrimage.

A person who does not pay attention to these causes has weak or incomplete faith because the one who informs us of these truths is the infallible revelation, whether in the Noble Quran or on the tongue of the Prophet, peace and blessings be upon him and his family. These are among the blessings of revelation, for our minds are not capable of reaching them independently, and some of these causes may even seem strange to some people. Spending money on pilgrimage and minor pilgrimage eliminates poverty, as the truthful one, peace and blessings be upon him and his family, tells us.

And the one who gives from his wealth and gives charity has done one of the causes of expanding provision because that is what the one who {does not speak from desire It is only a revelation revealed} has informed us.

From Abdullah ibn Masud, may Allah be pleased with him, who said: The Messenger of Allah, peace and blessings be upon him, said: (Alternate between pilgrimage and minor pilgrimage, for they eliminate poverty and sins as the bellows eliminates the impurities of iron, gold, and silver. And there is no reward for an accepted pilgrimage except Paradise).

An accepted pilgrimage is one that has fulfilled its rulings, so the pilgrimage occurred in accordance with what was required from the responsible person in the most complete manner. This is the meaning of an accepted pilgrimage.

Here, the Prophet, peace and blessings be upon him and his family, clarifies that one of the fruits of alternation between pilgrimage and minor pilgrimage is the elimination of poverty and sins as the bellows eliminates the impurities of iron, gold, and silver. Therefore, Imam Ibn Hibban titled this hadith by saying: The mention of pilgrimage and minor pilgrimage eliminating sins and poverty from Muslims through them.

And Imam Al-Tibi said in explaining the Prophet's, peace and blessings be upon him, saying: (For they eliminate poverty and sins): Its removal of poverty is like the increase of charity to wealth, meaning: Just as charity increases wealth and does not decrease it, for the Prophet, peace and blessings be upon him, swore on this when he said: (Charity does not decrease wealth), likewise the expenditure you spend on pilgrimage and minor pilgrimage eliminates poverty from you.

And Imam Al-Nasa'i narrated from Ibn Abbas, may Allah be pleased with them, who said: The Messenger of Allah, peace and blessings be upon him, said: (Alternate between pilgrimage and minor pilgrimage, for they eliminate poverty and sins as the bellows eliminates the impurities of iron).

So, among the deeds that Allah Almighty has made a key to sustenance is the consistency in Hajj and Umrah (i.e., performing Hajj and Umrah one after the other).

By the grace of Allah, this will be discussed under the following two headings:

a: The meaning of consistency in Hajj and Umrah

b: Two proofs of the consistency in Hajj and Umrah being the key to sustenance

a: The meaning of consistency in Hajj and Umrah:

Sheikh Abu al-Hasan al-Sindi writes about this:

"Make one follow the other, meaning when you perform Hajj, then perform Umrah, and when you finish Umrah, then prepare for Hajj, because these two come one after the other."

b: Two proofs of the consistency in Hajj and Umrah being the key to sustenance:

1: Imams Ahmad, Tirmidhi, Nasa'i, Ibn Khuzaymah, and Ibn Hibban have narrated from Abdullah ibn Mas'ud (may Allah be pleased with him), that he said: "The Messenger of Allah (peace and blessings be upon him) said:

'Follow up Hajj and Umrah, for they remove poverty and sins as the bellows remove impurities from iron, gold, and silver, and the reward for a Hajj Mabroor (accepted Hajj) is nothing but Paradise.'"

In this hadith, the Prophet (peace and blessings be upon him) informed the ummah that due to the consistency in Hajj and Umrah, they will gain the following two benefits:

1: Elimination of poverty and destitution

2: Erasure of sins

And it is known that the Prophet (peace and blessings be upon him) conveyed such matters through divine revelation. Allah Almighty says:

"And he does not speak from his own desire. It is only a revelation revealed."

Imam Ibn Hibban wrote the following title for this hadith:

"The mention of Hajj and Umrah removing sins and poverty from the Muslim through them."

Allama Tayyibi, in explaining the phrase writes:

"These two remove poverty just as charity increases wealth."

2: Imam Nasa'i narrated from Ibn Abbas (may Allah be pleased with them), that he said: "The Messenger of Allah (peace and blessings be upon him) said:

'Perform Hajj and Umrah consecutively, for they remove poverty and sins just as the bellows remove impurities from iron.'"

O you who desire relief from poverty and destitution! O you who seek forgiveness for sins! Hurry to perform Hajj and Umrah consecutively. If you have performed Umrah, prepare for Hajj, and if you have performed Hajj, strive to perform Umrah.

Note: In the case of severe crowding, for the sake of ease for first-time Hajj and Umrah performers, it is hoped from Allah Almighty that those who leave out consecutiveness will not be deprived of the reward and benefits of it. Insha'Allah.

Maintaining Family Ties

Among the reasons for invoking Allah's provision is maintaining family ties. The righteous predecessors used to maintain family ties, and they were rewarded for that by having their wealth grow and their numbers increase whenever they kept in touch. You will not find a family that maintains its ties in need.

Maintaining family ties is not limited to financial support; its concept is broader than that. It can be through financial support, helping with needs, preventing harm, a friendly demeanor, praying for them, and the comprehensive definition of maintaining family ties: providing as much good as possible and warding off as much harm as possible within one's ability.

Islam does not prohibit maintaining family ties even with disbelievers. If one has disbelieving relatives, they are commanded to be kind to them, as indicated by the verse: {Allah does not forbid you from those who do not fight you because of religion and do not expel you from your homes – from being righteous toward them and acting justly toward them. Indeed, Allah loves those who act justly}.

The reason for the revelation of this verse is that Asma bint Abi Bakr, may Allah be pleased with them, had a polytheist mother who wanted to maintain ties with her. She asked the Prophet, peace be upon him, saying, "My mother has come to me, and she is eager, should I maintain ties with my mother?" He said, "Yes, maintain ties with your mother."

This maintenance does not mean loving the disbeliever or compromising with them, as Allah says: {You will not find a people who believe in Allah and the Last Day having affection for those who oppose Allah and His Messenger, even if they were their fathers or their sons or their brothers or their kindred}. The faith of a person does not coexist with the love of Allah's enemies because loving someone excludes loving their enemy. It is not possible to love the believers and the enemies of Allah at the same time.

Imam Malik used this verse as evidence for opposing the innovators and avoiding their company. Imam Qurtubi commented on this, saying that the same applies to all people of injustice and aggression.

This means they deserve to be boycotted as well.

Ibn Kathir said: "They do not show affection to those who oppose, even if they are close relatives."

A person should maintain family ties even if they are disbelievers or sinners, inviting them to repentance and obedience to the best of their ability, making every effort in this. If they persist in what they are upon after advice, then boycotting them for the sake of Allah is maintaining ties with them, provided one makes every effort in advising them and then informing them that if they persist in what they are upon, they will be boycotted for that reason. They must be informed that the reason for the boycott is their enmity towards Allah and His Messenger, peace be upon him. Nevertheless, one should not cease praying for them in their absence, hoping they will return to the right path.

So, one of the means to gain sustenance is (maintaining family ties). The discussion on this topic, Insha'Allah, will be under the following four points:

a: The meaning of maintaining family ties

b: Six evidences of maintaining family ties being a key to sustenance

c: With whom and how should family ties be maintained?

d: The manner of maintaining family ties with the disobedient

a: The meaning of maintaining family ties:

In Arabic, the words used for maintaining family ties refers to relatives.

Two scholars' statements:

Hafiz Ibn Hajar writes:

Relatives refer to those who have mutual kinship, whether they are heirs to each other or not, or whether they are Mahram or not.

It is also said in the explanation of this that they are only Mahram relatives, but the first opinion is preferred because, based on this explanation, paternal and maternal cousins are excluded from due to not being Mahram, and this is not correct.

By maintaining family ties, according to Mulla Ali Qari, it means to do good to relatives by blood and marriage, to show compassion and sympathy towards them, and to take care and be considerate of their conditions.

b: Six evidences of maintaining family ties being a key to sustenance:

The mention of maintaining family ties as a cause of increased sustenance is found in several Hadiths and traditions. Six of them are as follows:

a: Imam Bukhari narrates from Hazrat Abu Huraira (Allah be pleased with him) that he said, "I heard the Messenger of Allah (peace and blessings of Allah be upon him) saying:

"Whoever wishes that his sustenance be expanded and his life span be extended, let him maintain his family ties."

2: Imam Bukhari narrates from Hazrat Anas bin Malik (Allah be pleased with him) that indeed the Messenger of Allah (peace and blessings of Allah be upon him) said:

"Whoever loves that his sustenance be expanded and his life span be extended, let him maintain his family ties."

The Messenger of Allah (peace and blessings of Allah be upon him) mentioned two good results achieved through maintaining family ties: the expansion of sustenance and an increase in lifespan. This is a clear offer made by the most truthful of all creatures, the beloved of Allah, Hazrat Muhammad (peace and blessings of Allah be upon him).

It should be noted that such offers are made not from his own accord, but through divine revelation. Therefore, anyone desiring these two fruits (expansion of sustenance and increase in lifespan) should plant the seed of maintaining family ties and will certainly obtain these fruits, God willing.

Imam Bukhari titled these hadiths as follows:

'The Chapter on Who is Given Increased Sustenance by Maintaining Family Ties'

Imam Ibn Hibban titled Hazrat Anas (Allah be pleased with him)'s hadith as:

'The Mention of a Comfortable Life in Security and Abundant Blessings in Sustenance for One Who Maintains Family Ties'

3. The Imams Ahmed, Tirmidhi, and Hakim narrate from Hazrat Abu Huraira (Allah be pleased with him) that he narrated from the Prophet (peace and blessings of Allah be upon him):

'Learn about your family relations so that you may maintain them. Indeed, maintaining family ties increases love in the family, wealth, and lifespan.'

The Messenger of Allah (peace and blessings of Allah be upon him) mentioned three benefits of maintaining family ties in this hadith, with one of them being an increase in wealth.

4. Imams Abdullah bin Ahmad, Bazzar, and Tabarani narrate from Hazrat Ali bin Abi Talib (Allah be pleased with him) that he narrated from the Prophet (peace and blessings of Allah be upon him):

'Whoever wishes that his life be extended, his sustenance be increased, and bad death be repelled, let him fear Allah and maintain his family ties.'

The Prophet (peace and blessings of Allah be upon him) mentioned that one who possesses two qualities—(fear of Allah) and (maintaining family ties)—will receive three benefits, one of which is the expansion of sustenance.

5. Imam Bukhari narrates from Hazrat Abdullah bin Umar (Allah be pleased with him) that he said:

'Whoever fears his Lord and maintains family ties, his life span is extended, his wealth is increased, and his family loves him.'

6. Allah, the Exalted, has placed such efficacy in maintaining family ties that even disobedient and bad people, if they maintain family ties, see an increase in their wealth and numbers in this world due to it. This is evidenced by the following hadith:

Imam Ibn Hibban narrates from Hazrat Abu Bakrah (Allah be pleased with him) that he narrated from the Prophet (peace and blessings of Allah be upon him):

"The quickest rewarded act of obedience is maintaining family ties. Even if a household is sinful, their wealth will increase, and their numbers will grow if they maintain ties. And no household that maintains family ties will ever be in need."

c: How and with What to Maintain Family Ties:

Some people think that maintaining family ties is only through wealth. This is an incomplete and flawed concept of maintaining family ties. The scope of maintaining family ties is much broader. The term (maintaining family ties) encompasses every effort to benefit relatives and keep harm away from them, whether it be through wealth or other means.

The Mercy to the Worlds (peace and blessings of Allah be upon him) has clearly explained the wide scope of maintaining family ties in the following phrase:

"Maintain your ties with your relatives, even if it is only through greeting them with Salaam."

Imam Ibn Abi Jamra writes: "Maintaining family ties is done through wealth, cooperation at times of need, efforts to remove distress, meeting with a smiling face, and through supplication.

The comprehensive concept of maintaining family ties is: to deliver all possible good and to keep away all possible harm."

d: The Nature and Method of Maintaining Family Ties with Disobedient and Bad People:

Many people are confused about the nature and method of maintaining family ties with disobedient and bad people. In their view, maintaining ties with such people means establishing friendly relations with them, joining their gatherings, becoming their eating and drinking companions, adopting a policy of indulgence and hypocrisy despite witnessing their disobedience and evil deeds, and smiling falsely and agreeing with them instead of getting angry for Allah's sake and stopping them from their wrongdoing. This way of maintaining family ties has no connection with Islam.

Someone might wonder if Islam has not prohibited doing good to disobedient and bad relatives.

In response, we say that Islam not only does not prohibit doing good to disobedient and bad relatives but also allows doing good to disbelievers. Allah the Exalted says:

"Allah does not forbid you from those who do not fight you because of religion and do not expel you from your homes, from being righteous toward them and acting justly toward them. Indeed, Allah loves those who act justly."

And this is supported by the hadith of Hazrat Asma bint Abi Bakr (Allah be pleased with him), that when her polytheist mother came to her, she asked the Prophet (peace and blessings of Allah be upon him):

"My mother has come and she wants me to maintain kinship with her. Should I maintain kinship with my mother?" The Prophet Muhammad (peace be upon him) said: "Yes, maintain kinship with your mother." But it is noteworthy that doing good to disbelievers and disobedient ones does not mean establishing friendly relations with them, participating in their gatherings to become their companion, or adopting a policy of flattery and hypocrisy with them despite witnessing their rebellion and defiance. (Doing good to disbelievers and disobedient ones) and (having heartfelt friendship and love for them) are two separate things. The same Allah who permitted (kindness to them) also prohibited (having heartfelt love) for those who disobey Allah and His Messenger (peace be upon him). Allah, the Almighty, says:

(You will not find people who believe in Allah and the Last Day having affection for those who oppose Allah and His Messenger, even if they were their fathers or their sons or their brothers or their relatives.)

Allama Razi writes in its commentary:

The heart in which faith and the love of the enemies of Allah cannot coexist because when a person loves someone, then with him, he does not love his enemies."

Imam Malik used this verse to argue for enmity and severing relations with the Qadariyyah sect.

Allama Qurtubi, commenting on Imam Malik's reasoning, writes:

"All those who commit injustice and excess are deserving of the treatment given to the people of the Qadariyyah sect."

Hafiz Ibn Kathir, in his commentary, writes:

"They (i.e., those who believe in Allah and the Last Day) do not have affection for those who disobey Allah and His Messenger (peace be upon him), even if they are their close relatives."

True and sincere kinship with disobedient and bad relatives means to strive earnestly to bring them to the path of goodness and save them from evil. These relatives, by abandoning the path of righteousness and following the path of wickedness, are indeed getting closer to the fire of Hell. What kind of kinship is it that a dear and close person is consciously or unconsciously preparing to become fuel for the fire of Hell, and his relative stands by as a silent spectator? Such a silent spectator is not one who maintains kinship, but certainly one who severs kinship (The silent spectator is actually severing kinship if he is silent).

The statement of the Prophet Muhammad (peace be upon him) that (stopping a tyrant brother from his oppression is helping him) is very effective and beneficial to clarify this reality. Imam Bukhari narrated from Anas (may Allah be pleased with him) that the Messenger of Allah (peace be upon him) said:

"Help your brother, whether he is an oppressor or oppressed."

A person asked:

"O Messenger of Allah (peace be upon him)! I help him when he is oppressed, but (tell me) how can I help him when he is an oppressor?"

The Prophet (peace be upon him) said:

"Prevent him from oppression, for indeed that is helping him."

Let's try to understand this with an example. Suppose someone's mother, sister, daughter, wife, or another relative is in the kitchen. Suddenly, a fire breaks out in the kitchen. Will someone who maintains kinship tolerate that their relative in the kitchen burns to ashes in the blazing fire while they silently watch? If someone who maintains kinship considers it necessary to make every effort to save their relative from the fire of this world, how can they be negligent and indifferent in saving their dear one from the fire of Hell? Here, it should also be noted that to bring disobedient and bad relatives to the path of righteousness and save them from the path of evil, if boycotting them is necessary, then boycotting them, i.e., severing ties with them, is kinship, and in such a situation, maintaining a relationship of friendship and love with them is severing kinship. Imam Ibn Abi Jamrah writes: "If (a relative) is a disbeliever or disobedient, then severing ties with them for the sake of Allah is kinship. However, before taking this step, one should make every effort to make them understand, and if preaching and advising them prove ineffective, inform them that severing ties is due to their persistence in disobedience. Even in the state of severing ties, continue to plead with Allah to guide them to the right path."

Spending in the Way of Allah

Among these reasons as well is spending in the way of Allah, the Blessed and Exalted: this is one of the keys to provision through which Allah's provision is invoked. Allah Almighty says: {And whatever you spend of anything [in Allah's cause], He will replace it; and He is the best of providers} [Saba: 39]. The recommended spending in religion includes spending on the poor, spending to support the religion of Allah, spending on acts of obedience, and spending on family and guests.

There are many evidences that spending in the way of Allah is one of the reasons for invoking Allah's provision, among them is His saying: {And whatever you spend of anything [in Allah's cause], He will replace it; and He is the best of providers} [Saba: 39]. This means: whatever you spend on what Allah has commanded you and permitted for you, He will replace it for you in this world with a substitute and in the Hereafter with reward and recompense as it is confirmed in the Hadith. It is not limited to reward in the Hereafter, but He also replaces it for you in this world, so spending is a reason for invoking provision.

One of the wives of the Prophet, peace be upon him, slaughtered a sheep. The Prophet, peace be upon him, asked her about the sheep and she said: "All of it has gone except its shoulder." The Prophet, peace be upon him, said: "Rather, all of it has remained except this shoulder," meaning that what you spend in the way of Allah remains for you, and its reward is stored with Allah Almighty as Allah Almighty said: {What is with you will perish, but what is with Allah is lasting} [Nahl: 96].

He also said, peace be upon him: "Three things I swear to, and mention - charity does not decrease wealth," so charity is a cause of blessing in what remains of wealth, and Allah replaces it for a person in this world besides the reward that remains for him in the Hereafter, {And whatever you spend of anything [in Allah's cause], He will replace it} [Saba: 39].

Bukhari narrated from Abu Huraira, may Allah be pleased with him, that the Prophet, peace be upon him, said: "Every day, two angels descend, and one of them says, 'O Allah, give to the one who spends a substitute,' and the other says, 'O Allah, give to the one who withholds, destruction.'"

Allah Almighty is Sovereign, Owner, Exalted, and Rich, so when He says, "Spend and I will replace it," by virtue of the promise, He obligates Himself to give this substitute. Allah has promised and said: {And whatever you spend of anything [in Allah's cause], He will replace it} [Saba: 39], and Allah's promise is true. If you are dealing with a rich person among humans, for example, and he says to you: "Throw your belongings into the sea, and I guarantee it," and you know from his character that he does not break promises and fulfills his word, you will trust that he will fulfill what he promised of this guarantee. Would you do this trust in his promise, and Allah Almighty has the highest example? Whoever spends has fulfilled what is a reason for obtaining the substitute because he has fulfilled the condition, and Allah Almighty has stipulated upon Himself and said: "Spend and I will spend on you," as the Prophet, peace be upon him, said: "Spend, Bilal, and do not fear from the One who owns the Throne any poverty," so this is a promise of replacement and compensation and substitute, so whoever fulfills the condition receives the substitute.

Whoever is stingy, the demise of wealth is necessary, and he did not fulfill what deserves the substitute.

So, His saying, the Blessed and Exalted: {And whatever you spend of anything [in Allah's cause], He will replace it} [Saba: 39] realizes the meaning of his saying, peace be upon him: "Every day, two angels descend, and one of them says, 'O Allah, give to the one who spends a substitute,' and the other says, 'O Allah, give to the one who withholds, destruction.'"

If a trader knows that some of his money is exposed to destruction, he will sell it on credit even to the poor. Suppose a trader sells fruits or vegetables, and this trader needs the profit he makes from this trade, and he stipulates in the sale that it must be immediate, meaning you must pay the money in cash. But if no one buys from him, and the goods are about to spoil, he will sell them on credit, because he is between losing the goods and selling them on credit. The wise person chooses to sell them on credit and says: "This is better than throwing them in the garbage," and when he sells them on credit, he will get the money even after a while. If he does not sell until it perishes, he is attributed to making a mistake, and if he gets a wealthy guarantor and does not sell to him, he is attributed to madness.

This means that this man wants to buy from him on credit, and if he does not buy the goods, they will spoil. Another wealthy man comes and tells the trader: "I guarantee and act as surety for the buyer that if he does not pay you, I will pay you the price of these goods," and this guarantor or surety is rich and trustworthy. In the Hadith: "Whoever is referred to a wealthy person, let him follow," so if he gets a wealthy guarantor and does not sell, this man is attributed to madness.

Each one of us does this and does not know that it is close to madness, for Allah Almighty guarantees replacement and that He will compensate those who spend in His way. Despite this, we find the general people taking the path of someone described as mad, and what a difference between a wealthy guarantor among humans and Allah

Almighty who is the Lord of the Throne, who is rich and does not need the servants, the Provider of strength and might.

Why do you not trust in the promise of Allah Almighty when He tells you in the Quran that He will replace for you, and you still insist on letting your goods perish and disappear without being rewarded for them, and without gaining any reward or price for them? Each one of us does this and does not know that it is close to madness, for all our wealth is in the sure exposure to demise. Spending on family and children is lending, and the wealthy guarantor is Allah the All-Knowing. He said: {And whatever you spend of anything [in Allah's cause], He will replace it} [Saba: 39], then He mortgaged to each one of us either land or orchard or mill or bath or any goods, so Allah Almighty gave you the amount from which you take your provision. This amount, whether it is a car or a machine or a factory or a shop or other, it is as if He says: "If you are not confident in my guarantee that I guarantee for you that I will replace for you, then place this mortgage before your eyes so that you are assured of the guarantee."

All the crafts that any of us has are but from the grace of Allah Almighty. Is this our property or the property of Allah? We own nothing at all, {and spend out of that in which He has made you successors} [Hadid: 7], and He says: {and give them from the wealth of Allah which He has given you} [Nur: 33], so the wealth in our hands is not truly ours but is a loan with us, and it is the property of Allah Almighty. With the guarantee, He commands you to spend, and He gives you a mortgage so that you are more assured, and you have this source of provision with you.

A person must have a craft or a source from which he gets money, and that is the property of Allah, and it is in the hand of the person by way of a loan, so it is as if it is mortgaged by what Allah has guaranteed of provision to have complete confidence. Despite this, he does not spend and lets his wealth perish without being rewarded or thanked.

Allah Almighty has confirmed His promise in this verse to those who spend with three affirmations: the first: the conditional form {And whatever you spend of anything [in Allah's cause], He will replace it} [Saba: 39], the second: making the answer a nominal sentence (He will replace it), the third: presenting the subject on the verbal predicate and said: (He will replace it) and did not say: so I will replace it for you.

The promise of Allah Almighty happens even if it is not coupled with these affirmations, so how about when it is confirmed by all these affirmations.

Among the evidences that spending is a cause of provision is His saying: {Satan threatens you with poverty and orders you to immorality, while Allah promises you forgiveness from Him and bounty. And Allah is all-Encompassing and Knowing} [Baqara: 268].

(He threatens you) means: he frightens you, saying: beware of spending or you will become poor.

(And orders you to immorality) means: stinginess, (while Allah promises you forgiveness from Him) for these sins (and bounty) meaning: in provision, and Ibn Attiyah said: forgiveness is the covering over His servants in this world and the Hereafter, and bounty is provision in this world, its expansion, and bliss in the Hereafter, and Allah Almighty has promised all this.

Ibn al-Qayyim, may Allah have mercy on him, said: Satan's promise of poverty is not out of compassion for him nor advice for him.

This means that when Satan tells you: do not spend, or you will become poor, he is not sincere in advice or wanting good for you; he is a clear enemy, and there is no solution with Satan except to take him as an enemy {Indeed, Satan is an enemy to you; so take him as an enemy} [Fatir: 6]. He is an enemy who cannot be dealt with leniency or kindness or gentleness; there is no way out in dealing with Satan except to treat him as a clear enemy, so do not trust any promise from his promises. When he tells you: do not spend, or you will become poor, do not trust his news, for he is not compassionate nor advising you. But Allah Almighty promises His servant forgiveness of his sins and bounty by replacing for him more than what he spent and many times over, either in this world or in both the world and the Hereafter.

It is reported in Sahih Muslim that Allah the Blessed and Exalted said: "O son of Adam! Spend, I will spend on you." It is also authentic from the Prophet, peace be upon him, that he said: "Indeed, Allah Almighty has people He chooses for His blessings for the benefit of His servants, and He keeps them as long as they give, but if they withhold, He takes them away and transfers them to others," or as he, peace be upon him, said.

So, the miser whom Allah gives of His wealth but does not spend on himself, his family, his children, the poor, and the needy, and wants to keep it, is poor. Ibn al-Qayyim said: the miser is poor and does not earn a reward for his poverty, and the poor person is better than him because the poor person earns a reward for his poverty, but this one is poor and does not earn a reward for his poverty. The poet describes the miserly: They were created but not for nobility, as if they were created but not created. They were given but did not give a successful hand, as if they were given but not given. In the Hadith: "Every day, two angels descend, and one of them says, 'O Allah, give to the one who spends a substitute,' and the other says, 'O Allah, give to the one who withholds, destruction,'" meaning destruction of his wealth either literally or metaphorically, either the wealth is lost or the blessing is removed from it, or he is compelled to spend it in what does not benefit him, or in things that anger Allah Almighty.

So, one of the means of sustenance is (spending in the way of Allah). This topic, insha'Allah, will be discussed under the following two headings:

a) The meaning of spending in the way of Allah

b) Six evidences that spending in the way of Allah is a cause of sustenance

a) The meaning of spending in the way of Allah:

Sheikh Ibn Ashur, in the commentary of the noble verse writes: "Spending means spending in a way that is preferred in religion, such as spending on the poor, and spending in the way of Allah for the support and aid of the religion."

b) Six evidences that spending in the way of Allah is a cause of sustenance:

Numerous verses and hadiths in the Qur'an and Sunnah clearly state that spending in the way of Allah, in addition to the rewards and recompense in the hereafter, also provides recompense and rewards in this world. Six such evidences are as follows:

a) Allah, the Lord of Glory, says:

(And whatever you spend [in the way of Allah], He will replace it, and He is the best of providers.)

In his commentary, Hafiz Ibn Kathir writes: Allah commands and permits you to spend, and whatever you spend, He will reward you for it in this world and grant you rewards and recompense in the Hereafter, as proven by the hadith...

Allama Razi writes: Allah's statement confirms the noble statement of the Prophet (peace be upon him): "There is no day on which the servants of Allah rise... [the hadith]

The matter is that Allah, the Exalted and the Sovereign, the Owner of treasures and independent of the universe, when He says, "Spend, and its recompense is My responsibility," then because of His promise, providing the recompense becomes obligatory upon Him.

So, whoever spends (in the way of Allah) fulfills the condition for receiving the recompense, and whoever does not spend, surely their wealth will perish. They did not fulfill the condition for receiving recompense for their wealth, so their wealth will perish without recompense.

Allama Razi further clarifies this with an example:

"A merchant knows that some of his goods are going to spoil and perish. He will sell these goods on credit, even if the buyer is poor. He will say that it is better to get some compensation after a while rather than letting the goods spoil. If he does not sell those goods on credit and they perish, everyone will say that he made a mistake. Then, if in the case of selling on credit, a wealthy guarantor is available and he still does not sell the goods, and they perish, he will be considered foolish. If a thing is kept as a mortgage and a mortgage deed is written, and he still does not sell, he will be deemed insane."

Allama Razi further writes:

"Those who adopt this approach (i.e., those who do not spend in the way of Allah) are oblivious to the fact that their policy is close to madness. All our wealth is definitely going to perish. Spending on family and children is giving a loan. The guarantor of this loan is Allah, the Almighty, who said: 'And whatever you spend [in the way of Allah], He will replace it.'

Then this is also worth considering, that Allah has kept something or the other as a mortgage with everyone, such as land, gardens, a mill, a bathhouse, or some beneficial thing because everyone has some source of livelihood. All these things actually belong to Allah and are given to humans as a loan. These things are as if mortgaged by Allah for the responsibility of providing sustenance so that people have complete certainty about receiving sustenance from Allah, but despite all this, people (i.e., many people) do not spend their wealth (according to Allah's command) and are deprived of reward and appreciation, they let it be destroyed."

Warning:

An extremely noteworthy point in the above-mentioned noble verse is that for the firmness and strength of the promise made by Allah to provide recompense for those who spend in His way, the following three emphases have been made:

1. The use of the conditional phrase for the statement of the promise.

2. The use of the nominal sentence for the statement of the condition's consequence.

3. The precedence of the subject over the predicate in the nominal sentence.

And these three emphases indicate how serious Allah is about fulfilling His promise. And Allah is such that even without emphasis, there is no doubt about the fulfillment of His promise.

(And who is more faithful to his covenant than Allah?)

2. Allah says:

(Satan threatens you with poverty and commands you to immorality, while Allah promises you forgiveness from Him and bounty, and Allah is all-encompassing and all-knowing.)

In the commentary of this verse, Abdullah ibn Abbas (may Allah be pleased with him) stated: "Two things are from Allah and two are from Satan. He (Satan) says: Do not spend your wealth, keep it to yourself, you will need it and he commands you to immorality. (In contrast) Allah promises you forgiveness from Himself and and an increase in sustenance."

In the commentary of the verse, Qadhi Ibn Atiyah writes:

"(Forgiveness) means covering the faults of the servants in this world and the hereafter, and (bounty) means having sustenance in this world, experiencing its abundance and expansion, and receiving blessings in the hereafter. Allah has promised all these things to those who spend."

Imam Ibn Qayyim writes in his commentary:

"(Upon spending by a servant) Allah promises the forgiveness of his sins and assures him of His bounty, that He will grant him much more in this world or in both this world and the Hereafter than what he spent."

3: Imam Muslim narrates from Abu Huraira (may Allah be pleased with him) that the Holy Prophet (peace be upon him) said:

"Allah, Blessed and Exalted, said: 'O son of Adam! Spend, and I will spend on you.'"

Allahu Akbar! What an absolute guarantee and definitive assurance for those who spend in the way of the Holy Lord!

How easy, simple, and certain a way to obtain sustenance!

The servant spends in the way of Allah, and He spends on him. Moreover, when a poor, humble, and needy servant spends in His way according to his capacity, then the Owner of the treasures, the King of kings, the Appreciative Allah, will spend on him according to His grandeur, greatness, and majesty.

Imam Nawawi writes:

"Allah the Exalted's noble command {Spend, and I will spend on you} is the explanation of the verse {And whatever you spend of anything (in Allah's cause), He will replace it}, and it encourages spending in the ways of goodness and gives the glad tidings of the best recompense by Allah's grace."

4: Imam Bukhari narrates from Abu Huraira (may Allah be pleased with him) that indeed the Holy Prophet (peace and blessings be upon him) said:

"There is not a day that people wake up in it except that two angels descend. One of them says, 'O Allah, give to the one who spends a good replacement,' and the other says, 'O Allah, give destruction to the one who withholds.'"

In this hadith, the Holy Prophet (peace and blessings be upon him) informed the Ummah that for those who spend in the way of Allah, every morning an angel prays to Allah to grant them a replacement for the spent wealth. (Khalaf) refers to... as Mulla Ali Qari stated,... a great and good replacement, or it refers to compensation in this world and reward in the Hereafter, as mentioned in Allah's noble verse: {And whatever you spend of anything}.

It should also be known that the prayers of the angels are accepted in the Divine presence, because they do not pray for anyone without His permission. Allah the Exalted says:

{And they cannot intercede except for him with whom He is pleased. And they stand in awe for fear of Him.}

5: Imam Bayhaqi narrates from Abu Huraira (may Allah be pleased with him) that he narrated from the Holy Prophet (peace and blessings be upon him) that the Holy Prophet (peace and blessings be upon him) said:

"Spend, Bilal, and do not fear from the Owner of the Throne any decrease."

What a strong and firm guarantee of sustenance for the one who spends in the way of Allah!

Is it possible that the one who spends in the way of Allah might be left helpless and in need by the Lord of the Mighty Throne and become a victim of poverty and destitution? By the honor of the Lord of Glory, this is absolutely not possible.

Mulla Ali Qari writes in the explanation of the hadith:

"Do you fear that the Lord who manages the heavens and the earth will waste you? Do you fear that He who encompasses His mercy over all the inhabitants of the heavens and the earth, whether they are believers or disbelievers, birds or beasts, will disappoint you and reduce your sustenance?"

6: There are numerous incidents in the books of hadith, biography, translations, and history that indicate Allah has granted the best reward in this world to those who spend in His way. At this point, by the grace of Allah, I will present one such incident:

Imam Muslim narrates from Abu Huraira (may Allah be pleased with him) that he reported from the Holy Prophet (peace and blessings be upon him) that the Prophet (peace and blessings be upon him) said:

"While a man was in a barren land, he heard a voice from a cloud saying:

'Water the garden of so-and-so.'

The cloud moved aside and poured its water into a valley. A stream from those streams absorbed all the water. The man followed the water and saw a man standing in his garden, directing the water into the garden with his shovel. The man asked him:

'O servant of Allah! What is your name?'

He replied: 'So-and-so,' which was the same name he had heard from the cloud.

The gardener said: 'O servant of Allah! Why did you ask about my name?'"

He began to say: "The water of this cloud came from a voice I heard within it: 'Irrigate the garden of such and such a man.' And that was your name. So, what do you do in this garden?"

He replied: "Since you have told me this, (I will also tell you about myself), my practice is that I distribute one-third of the garden's produce as charity, one-third I and my family consume, and one-third I spend on the development of the garden."

And another narration says: "One-third is given to the poor, the beggars, and the travelers."

Imam Nawawi writes:

"This hadith shows the virtue of giving charity, showing kindness to the poor and travelers, eating from one's own earnings, and spending on one's family."

The essence is that one of the keys to sustenance is spending in the way of Allah. Allah, the Almighty, grants those who spend in His way much more in this world than what they have been given, and the reward and recompense in the Hereafter are separate.

Spending on Those Who Devote Themselves to Acquiring Islamic Knowledge

[Spending on Good People, Especially Students of Religious Knowledge]

Among the reasons for drawing and invoking provision from Allah, Glorified and Exalted be He, is what Anas ibn Malik, may Allah be pleased with him, narrated: (There were two brothers during the time of the Messenger of Allah, peace and blessings be upon him. One of them used to come to the Prophet, peace and blessings be upon him - meaning to seek knowledge - and the other practiced a trade - meaning to earn a living for both of them. The one who practiced the trade complained about his brother to the Prophet, peace and blessings be upon him, so the Prophet, peace and blessings be upon him, said to him: Perhaps you are provided for because of him).

It is as if he is saying: Perhaps you are provided for by his blessing, not by your effort, so do not boast about your craft to him; because he is devoted to the path of Allah. Many of the people of goodness are unable to earn a living due to their dedication to knowledge and similar pursuits. Therefore, whoever spends on them receives provision not only to take it for himself but also to give to others and to donate from it to his deserving brothers. He is like a distributing agent whom Allah provides with provision so that he may give. If he stops giving charity to them in order to save money for his children, for example, the Prophet, peace and blessings be upon him, said:

(Indeed, Allah has chosen people whom He blesses with His favors for the benefit of His servants, and He keeps them as long as they give, but if they withhold, He takes them away and transfers them to others).

So, among the means of sustenance is spending on those who dedicate themselves to acquiring Islamic knowledge. The details in this regard are as follows:

Evidence:

Imam Tirmidhi and Imam Hakim narrated from Hazrat Anas bin Malik (may Allah be pleased with him) that he said: "There were two brothers during the time of the Messenger of Allah (peace be upon him). One of them used to attend the Prophet (peace be upon him) for knowledge, while the other worked for his livelihood. The one who worked complained about his brother to the Prophet (peace be upon him). The Prophet (peace be upon him) said: 'Perhaps you are being provided sustenance through him.'"

The Messenger of Allah (peace be upon him) explained to the one who was striving for livelihood and complained about his brother who was engaged in seeking knowledge, that it is not right to show favor over his brother. The worker thought he was earning through his efforts and that his brother was merely consuming without working, but he did not know that the sustenance he was receiving might be due to the blessings of his brother who was dedicated to seeking knowledge.

Explanation of the Hadith by Two Scholars:

1. **Mulla Ali Qari:** He writes in the commentary of the Prophet's (peace be upon him) statement "Perhaps you are being provided sustenance through him" that it is in the passive form. It means that the hope or suspicion is that the reason for the sustenance you receive is not your skill or craftsmanship,

but rather the blessings from your brother who is engaged in seeking knowledge. Therefore, do not show favor to him based on your own skills.

1. **Allama Taibi**: He discusses two possibilities regarding the use of "La-Alla" in the Prophet's (peace be upon him) statement:

-   One possibility is that it signifies certainty or admonishment from the Prophet (peace be upon him), similar to another hadith: "You are only provided sustenance because of your weak ones."

-   The other possibility is that it is meant to encourage the listener to reflect and be prompted towards justice and fairness.

Statements of Two Scholars:

1. Some scholars of the Ummah have also said that those who dedicate themselves to acquiring Islamic knowledge are included in the following verse:

{For the poor who are confined in the way of Allah, unable to travel in the land. The ignorant person considers them to be rich due to their abstinence. You recognize them by their appearance. They do not beg from people insistently. And whatever you spend of good, indeed Allah is Knowing of it.}

2. Allama Ghazali writes:

"You should ensure that your alms reach such people who increase the value of alms, like spending on people of knowledge, because it will help them in acquiring knowledge. If the intention is correct, then knowledge is the highest form of worship. Imam Abdullah bin

Mubarak used to give his charity to scholars. When he was told, 'Include others in the distribution of your charity,' he replied, 'After the position of Prophethood, I do not know of any position that is higher or better than that of scholars.' If a scholar's heart becomes occupied with fulfilling his own needs, he will not be free to seek knowledge or advance in learning. It is preferable to relieve them for the sake of acquiring knowledge."

Summary of the Discussion:

The person who desires sustenance should spend his wealth on those who have dedicated themselves to acquiring Islamic knowledge.

Showing Kindness to the Weak

Among the keys to provision is kindness to the poor. Imam Bukhari narrated from Mus'ab bin Sa'd, may Allah be pleased with him, who said: (Sa'd, may Allah be pleased with him, saw that he had superiority over those below him, so the Messenger of Allah, peace and blessings be upon him, said: "Are you not given victory and provision except because of your weak ones?"), meaning: Does Allah not grant you victory and provision except for the sake of the weak?

The weak are the ones with the true favor, not those who give charity to them and help them. Whoever wants Allah to grant him victory over his enemies and provide for him should honor the weak and be kind to them. The Prophet, peace and blessings be upon him, explained that whoever wants to please him should please the poor and needy. He said in the hadith: (Seek me among your weak ones - meaning: Whoever wants to please me and be kind to me should be kind to the weak - seek me among your weak ones, for you are only provided for and given victory because of your weak ones).

So, among the means of sustenance is showing kindness to the weak, the frail, the helpless, and those in need.

Two Evidences:

1. Imam Bukhari narrates from Musab bin Saad (may Allah be pleased with him), who said:

"Saad (may Allah be pleased with him) thought that he had superiority over those weaker than him, so the Messenger of Allah (peace be upon him) said: 'Are you not helped and provided sustenance except through your weak ones?'"

"So whoever wishes that Allah grants him support and opens the doors of sustenance in the face of his enemies, he should honor and show kindness to the weak, frail, and helpless Muslims."

2. In another hadith, the Prophet (peace be upon him) said that whoever wishes to please Allah should show kindness to the weak among the Ummah. Imams Ahmad, Abu Dawood, Tirmidhi, Nasai, Ibn Hibban, and Hakim narrate from Abu Darda (may Allah be pleased with him), who said: "I heard the Messenger of Allah (peace be upon him) say: 'Seek me in your weak ones, for you are provided sustenance and supported through your weak ones.'"

Explanation of the Prophet's (peace be upon him) Statement:

In explaining the Prophet's (peace be upon him) statement "Seek me in your weak ones," Mulla Ali Qari writes:

"Try to gain my pleasure by showing kindness to your poor ones. Through this, you will receive sustenance and support."

Translation:

Whoever pleases and satisfies the Beloved of Allah, the Most Merciful and Compassionate (peace be upon him) by showing kindness to the poor and weak, their Lord, the Compassionate and the Merciful, will be pleased and happy with them. He will support them against their enemies and open the doors of sustenance through His grace.

O Generous Lord! Do not deprive us of this blessing. Indeed, You are Generous and Noble.

Emigrating in the Way of Allah

[Migration for the Sake of Allah]

Among the reasons for the increase in provision is migration for the sake of Allah Almighty. Migration is moving from the land of disbelief to the land of faith, as those who migrated from Makkah to Madinah did. Allah Almighty says: {And whoever migrates for the cause of Allah will find in the earth many locations and abundance} [An-Nisa:100], meaning if one migrates from one country to another, they will find in the land they migrated to many blessings and abundance, which will be a cause for their enemies' humiliation who were in their original country. This is because when someone leaves their country and settles in another, the news of their success reaches their original country and causes their enemies to feel ashamed of their mistreatment towards them, resulting in their humiliation. The phrase "and abundance" means abundance in provision, or abundance from misguidance to guidance, from poverty to wealth. Malik said that abundance refers to the abundance of land.

The world has witnessed the truth of this promise and continues to witness it. The matter of those who migrated to Madinah from the companions of the Prophet Muhammad, peace and blessings be upon him, is well-known to anyone with even the slightest connection to Islamic history. When they left their homes, wealth, and possessions for migration for the sake of Allah Almighty, Allah compensated them by granting them the keys to Syria, Persia, and Yemen. He granted them the palaces of Syria, the white palace of Al-Mada'in, and opened the doors of Sana'a for them. He subjected them to the treasures of Caesar and Khosrau.

So, the summary of the interpretation of this verse, as stated by Al-Razi, is: O human being! If you say you dislike migrating from your homeland due to fear of facing hardship and distress in travel, do not fear, for Allah Almighty will grant you immense and great blessings in your migration that will be a cause of humiliation for your enemies and a cause of your abundant livelihood.

Thus, moving and striving on earth to seek lawful provision is not blameworthy. Allah has promised those who migrate for His sake with provision and recompense, but this migration should not be forbidden, such as the current reversed migration trend. Instead of migrating from the lands of disbelief to the land of Islam, now people are migrating from Muslim lands to the lands of disbelief! Who commands migration to the land of disbelief, Allah or Satan? Satan. Whoever migrates to the land of disbelief is obeying Satan and disobeying the Merciful Almighty, except for those who are excused in exceptional cases. However, most people do so only for worldly gains, which they obtain there but without blessings, and the provision is tainted with doubts or prohibitions.

Thinking about traveling to the lands of disbelief is destructive. Whoever commands migration from Muslim lands to the lands of disbelief for the sake of worldly gains is Satan, and this is not permissible except for those excused. Allah Almighty commands those in the lands of disbelief to leave for the lands of Muslims. The migrant may suffer in this world, but his religion will be safe. Who can claim that there is safety in religion there? It is a religious trial, deviation from the guidance of Islam, as is well known.

In summary the reasons for attracting the provision of Allah Almighty, which are: seeking forgiveness and repentance through words and deeds, piety, reliance on Allah, dedicating oneself to the worship of Allah Almighty, continuity between pilgrimage and Umrah, maintaining kinship ties, spending for the sake of Allah Almighty, spending on good people especially seekers of religious knowledge, kindness to the weak, and migration for the sake of Allah Almighty, which is moving from the land of disbelief to the land of faith, seeking the pleasure of Allah Almighty according to what Allah has prescribed.

Muslims across the globe should adhere to these reasons to attain provision, for all good lies in adhering to what the Creator Almighty has prescribed, and all evil lies in turning away from it.

What is with Allah cannot be obtained through disobedience, but it is obtained through obedience. He Almighty says: {O you who have believed, respond to Allah and to the Messenger when he calls you to that which gives you life. And know that Allah intervenes between a man and his heart and that to Him you will be gathered} [Al-Anfal:24], and He says: {And whoever turns away from My remembrance - indeed, he will have a depressed life, and We will gather him on the Day of Resurrection blind. He will say, "My Lord, why have you raised me blind while I was [once] seeing?" [Allah] will say, "Thus did Our signs come to you, and you forgot them; and thus will you this Day be forgotten} [Taha:125-126].

And may Allah's blessings and peace be upon our Prophet Muhammad, and upon his family, companions, and followers, and blessed them. The last of our supplication is that praise be to Allah, Lord of the worlds.

I say this and seek Allah's forgiveness for me and you.

Glory be to You, O Allah, our Lord, and praise be to You. I bear witness that there is no deity but You. I seek Your forgiveness and repent to You.

So, among the means of sustenance is emigrating in the way of Allah. The details in this regard are as follows:

A: The Concept of Emigration in the Way of Allah

Statements of Two Scholars:

1. Imam Raghib Isfahani writes:

"Leaving the land of disbelief for the land of faith is like emigrating from Makkah to Madinah."

2. Sayed Muhammad Rashid Rida states that emigration must be genuinely (i.e., purely) for the sake of Allah. The purpose of emigrating should be to establish the religion according to Allah's command and to support the believers against the disbelievers who oppress and mistreat them.

B: Evidence That Emigrating in the Way of Allah is a Means of Sustenance:

The following verse indicates that emigration in the way of Allah is a means of sustenance:

{And whoever emigrates for the sake of Allah will find much refuge and abundance in the earth.}

This noble verse describes two rewards for emigration in the way of Allah:

- The first reward: "much refuge"

- The second reward: "abundance"

Explanation of "much refuge":

As explained by Alama Razi, it means: "One who leaves his city for the sake of Allah will find goodness and blessings in the new city. This will be a cause of disgrace and humiliation for the people of the former city, as when the news of the emigrant's circumstances and dealings in the new place reaches the people of his former city, they will feel ashamed of their mistreatment and experience a sense of disgrace and dishonor."

Meaning of abundance and expansion in sustenance.

"The meaning is: Abundance from misguidance to guidance, and from poverty to wealth."

Imam Malik states: means the expanse of cities.

Allama Qurtubi comments on these interpretations: "Imam Malik's interpretation is closest to the eloquence of the Arabic language, as the expansiveness of land and dwellings leads to abundant sustenance, relief from worries, and other forms of ease."

In all three interpretations of the verse, whether directly or indirectly, there is a promise of expansion and abundance in sustenance due to emigration in the way of Allah. The promise of Allah, the Almighty, is true and just:

{Indeed, the promise of Allah is true, but most of them do not know.}

And He does not break His promise:

{The promise of Allah is not to be broken. Allah does not break His promise, but most people do not know.}

(iii): Testimony of World History:

World history attests to the truth of this promise, and today the veracity of this promise remains evident. Even those with a basic knowledge of Islamic history are aware that when the Companions of the Prophet (may Allah be pleased with them) emigrated for the sake of Allah, leaving behind their relatives, homes, possessions, and wealth in Makkah, Allah, the Sovereign of the Kingdom, granted them the keys to the treasures of the land of Syria, Iran, and Yemen. He made them the masters of the red palaces of Syria and the white palaces of Ctesiphon. He opened the gates of Sana'a for them and laid the treasures of the Byzantine and Sassanian empires at their feet.

Allama Razi summarizes the interpretation of the verse as follows:

"The essence of the verse is as if it is saying: 'O human!

If you dislike emigration from your homeland due to the fear of enduring the hardships and difficulties of living abroad, then remove this apprehension from your mind and heart. Where you emigrate to, Allah will grant you such abundant blessings and elevated status that those who drove you out of your homeland will feel humiliation and disgrace upon seeing your condition. Emigration will become a cause for the expansion and abundance of your sustenance.'"

Making the Hereafter One's Primary Focus

One of the means of sustenance in this world is for a person to (make the Hereafter his primary focus and ultimate goal). The discussion regarding this is outlined under the following two headings:

A: Three Arguments

B: Two Points Regarding These Arguments

A: Three Arguments:

1. Imam Tirmidhi narrated from Hazrat Anas bin Malik (may Allah be pleased with him), who said: The Messenger of Allah (peace be upon him) said:

"Whoever makes the Hereafter his concern, Allah will place contentment in his heart, will arrange his scattered affairs, and the world will come to him, albeit reluctantly... [Hadith]."

In the narration of Imam Bazzar:

"Whoever's intention is the Hereafter, Allah, Blessed and Exalted, will place contentment in his heart, will arrange his scattered affairs, will remove poverty from between his eyes, and the world will come to him, while it is..."

"Rāghimatun, so he neither wakes up except in wealth, nor goes to bed except in wealth"... [Hadith].

"Whoever has the Hereafter as his intention, Allah the Blessed and Exalted will place wealth in his heart, arrange his scattered affairs, remove poverty from between his eyes (i.e., from his forehead), and the world will come to him in a state of humiliation and insignificance; thus, he wakes up in wealth and goes to bed in wealth"... [Hadith].

2. Imam Ahmad and Imam Ibn Majah narrated from Hazrat Zaid bin Thabit (may Allah be pleased with him), who said: "I heard the Messenger of Allah (peace be upon him) say:

"And whoever makes the Hereafter his intention, Allah will arrange his affairs for him, will place wealth in his heart, and the world will come to him, albeit reluctantly."

In the narration of Imam Tabarani, instead of (JAMAA ALLAHU LAHU AMRAHU), the words are (WA YAKFEEHI DAI'ATUHU) (i.e., his means of livelihood will suffice him).

3. Imam Ibn Majah narrated from Hazrat Abdullah (bin Mas'ud) (may Allah be pleased with him), who said: "I heard your noble Prophet (peace be upon him) say:

"Whoever makes all his concerns focus on one concern: the concern for the Hereafter, Allah will suffice him from the concerns of this world. And whoever's concerns are dispersed among the affairs of this world, Allah will not care in which valley he perishes."

Meaning of making the Hereafter the focus:

Making the Hereafter and the Resurrection one's intention, goal, and target does not mean that one should not make effort for one's livelihood; rather, it means to strive within the bounds of Shariah, but the primary aim, goal, and target should be the Hereafter. One should not jeopardize the Hereafter while striving to improve and enhance the world.

Acting on the Book of Allah

One of the means of sustenance is that (one acts according to the Book revealed by Allah).

By divine grace, the discussion in this regard will be under the following three headings:

A: Proof

Divine command:

(And if they (i.e., the People of the Book) had established the Torah and the Gospel and what had been revealed to them from their Lord, they would certainly have eaten from above them and from below their feet. Among them is a moderate community, but many of them are evil in their deeds.)

B: Three points regarding the proof:

Four interpretations of the scholars:

"It is the Qur'an (Kareem)."

Allah says: "If they (i.e., the People of the Book) had acted upon the Furqan (i.e., the Qur'an Kareem), which was revealed to them and which (Prophet) Muhammad (peace be upon him) brought."

"(What was revealed to them from their Lord) i.e., the Qur'an (Kareem)."

"(What was revealed to them from their Lord) from the Qur'an Majid, which confirms their books."

2: The meanings of establishing the Torah, the Gospel, and (what was revealed by Allah):

Statements of six commentators:

1: "Their (establishing the Torah) means acting according to it."

2: "If they acted upon what is in the Torah and the Gospel, and what was revealed to them in the Furqan (i.e., the Qur'an Majid)."

3: "To establish something means to fulfill its rights. Establishing the Torah and the Gospel means fulfilling their rights with knowledge and practice."

4: "(Establishing something) means to set it up. (Establishing) is used metaphorically to mean not wasting it, because a wasted thing is left lying around."

5: "If the People of the Book obeyed Allah and established their book by acting upon what is contained in it..."

6: "The meaning of establishing these books is that they would believe in the correct beliefs contained in them and act upon the correct laws, high morals, and excellent ethics."

Statements of seven commentators:

1: "Allah would send down heavy rain from the sky upon them, and the earth would bring forth its blessings for them."

2: It is written: "They would eat from the blessings of the earth beneath their feet, which includes the grains, plants, fruits, and other edibles that the earth produces."

3: "If the People of the Book adhered to the commandments of the Torah, the Gospel, and the Qur'an Kareem, they would have eaten from above and below, meaning that Allah would have handed over the world to them."

4: "The mention of (from above) and (from below) is to exaggerate the abundance and variety of sustenance available to them, and the ease in obtaining means of livelihood."

5: "The generality of the means of sustenance means that they would have been provided sustenance from every direction."

6: "It has been clarified in other places that (the expansion and abundance of sustenance through adherence to the Books of Allah) is not specific to them (i.e., the People of the Book)."

We do not need to say that this condition of Allah is not specific to the People of the Book. More deserving of this condition are those upon whom the Qur'an was revealed and who call themselves Muslims. Their religion explicitly commands them to believe in their revealed book and the books revealed before it. They must fully adhere to the Shari'ah revealed to them and follow the commands from the earlier Shari'ahs that Allah has retained in their Shari'ah. In the entire Islamic world, Muslims suffering from hunger, disease, fear, and poverty are more deserving of benefiting from this conditional promise than the People of the Book. Allah's conditional promise is established and the path towards it is clear. If only they would use their intellect.

The summary of the discussion is that Allah stated for the People of the Book that if they acted upon the commands of the Torah, the Gospel, and the Qur'an Kareem, He would open the doors of sustenance for them from above and below. The same promise is for the people of Islam: if they adhere to the pure and sacred Qur'an revealed by Allah, He will grant them abundant sustenance through blessings and mercy from the heavens and the earth. May the Lord Almighty grant us and our descendants the success to benefit from this magnificent offer. Ameen, O Ever-Living, O Sustainer.

C: Warning:

Three points to keep in mind regarding (establishing the Torah, the Gospel, and the Qur'an Kareem):

i: Belief in the divine revelation of all three books.

ii: Acting upon the agreed-upon matters stated in all three books.

iii: In case of any disagreement among the Qur'an Kareem, the Torah, and the Gospel, accept and act upon what is mentioned in the Qur'an Kareem, because the Qur'an Kareem is the book that abrogates all previous books.

Excellence (Ihsan)

One of the means of sustenance is (excellence). Please see the details below under the following two headings:

A: Proof

B: Three points regarding the proof

A: Proof:

Divine Revelation:

{For those who do good, there is good in this world, and the home of the Hereafter is better. And the home of the righteous is indeed excellent.}

B: Three points regarding the proof:

In the above-mentioned verse, Allah has promised a reward in this world for those who practice (excellence). In this context, consider the following three points:

1: Meaning of (excellence):

The name of complying with all the commandments of Allah Almighty is "excellence." These commandments may relate to the person's own self or to other people. Imam Ibn Qayyim writes:

"At this place, 'excellence' means to perform the commanded action, whether it is kindness towards people or towards oneself."

2: By "good in this world," it means:

The statements of four commentators:

"It is good provision."

"(Good) is their reward in this world for their kindness, and for them in the hereafter is what is better than it."

"A broad provision, a pleasant life, peace of mind, security, and happiness."

"And 'good in this world' is a pure life, and besides that, the worldly life's beauty granted to them by Allah Almighty along with the blessing of faith."

3: Another statement of Allah Almighty:

"Say, 'O My servants who have believed, fear your Lord. For those who have done good in this world, there is good.'"

The conclusion of the discussion is that those who comply with all the commandments related to their Lord and other people's rights, meaning the rights of Allah and the rights of people, Allah Almighty grants them "good" in this world, which includes a broad provision, a pleasant life, peace of mind, security, and happiness, before the hereafter. Furthermore, the Merciful Lord has mentioned this promise twice in a single statement, whereas for the certainty and definitiveness of any promise, Allah Almighty's one statement is enough.

"Know that the promise of Allah is true, but most of them do not know."

Therefore, those seeking provision should strive diligently, eagerly, and with full attention to comply with all the commandments of the Generous Lord. May Allah Almighty grant us and our generations the ability to do so. Indeed, He is Near and Responsive.

Faith and Righteous Deeds

One of the means of sustenance is (the righteous deeds of the believers). Please see the following details under two headings:

A: Two Evidences

B: Eight Points Regarding These Evidences

A: Two Evidences:

1: Statement of Allah Almighty:

"Whoever does a good deed, whether male or female, and is a believer, We will surely grant them a pure life, and We will surely reward them according to the best of what they used to do."

2: Three Narrations:

"Indeed, Allah does not wrong a believer regarding any good deed; he is given something for it in this world, and he will be rewarded for it in the Hereafter."

"Indeed, Allah does not wrong a believer regarding any good deed; he is rewarded with provision in this world, and he will be rewarded for it in the Hereafter."

"Indeed, when the disbeliever does a good deed, he is given some provision from this world because of it. As for the believer, Allah stores his good deeds for him in the Hereafter and provides him with sustenance in this world because of his obedience."

B: Eight Points Regarding These Evidences:

1: Four Statements Regarding the Noble Verse:

"A pure life" and a better reward for his deeds in the Hereafter.

"A pure life" encompasses all forms of comfort received from every direction.

From Ibn Abbas (may Allah be pleased with him) and a group of scholars, it is narrated that this refers to "pure and lawful provision."

From Ali (may Allah be pleased with him), it is narrated that this refers to "contentment." This interpretation is also stated by Ibn Abbas, Ikrimah, and Wahb ibn Munabbih.

Ibn Abbas (may Allah be pleased with him) also interpreted this as (happiness). The imams Hasan, Mujahid, and Qatadah have stated that (the purity and cleanliness of life are only in Paradise). Imam Dhahak stated: "It is (the lawful provision and the ability to worship in the world)." Imam Dhahak also said: "It is (to do good deeds and to have an open heart for them)." According to Hafiz Ibn Kathir, the correct view is that (a pure life) encompasses all these things.

"We will surely grant them a pure life" refers to peace of mind, tranquility of the soul, protection from things that disturb the heart, and lawful provision from Allah given in ways beyond one's imagination.

In a pure life, lawful provision, contentment, true honor, peace and tranquility, richness of the heart, love of Allah, and delight are all included. The meaning is that not only will the hereafter be prosperous and peaceful due to faith and righteous deeds, but the worldly life will also be spent in comfort and ease.

In this noble verse, every Muslim (man and woman) is given good news that after having faith, whoever acts according to the Quran and

Sunnah, Allah will grant them (comfort and happiness and ample lawful provision) in this world and will give them a much better reward for their righteous deeds on the Day of Resurrection.

2: A Question and Its Answer Regarding the Noble Verse:

Regarding this noble verse, Allama Razi raised a question and answered it himself. He writes:

Question: In "Whoever does a good deed" the word "whoever" gives a general meaning, (i.e., it includes both male and female), so what is the benefit of mentioning the female later (i.e., why did Allah say "male or female")?

Answer: Indeed, this verse promises the granting of blessings, and to firmly establish the certainty of such a promise and to remove any doubt of its specificity (to any one gender), emphasizing it is one of the great proofs of mercy and kindness.

3: The Emphatic Promise of Granting a Pure Life:

Allah has promised to grant (a pure life) based on faith and righteous deeds with emphatic expression (We will surely grant them). This includes (lam) (of emphasis) and (nun) (of heavy emphasis). Even without emphasis, Allah does not break His promise.

"Indeed, Allah does not break His promise."

He is the most fulfilling of promises.

"And who is more faithful to his promise than Allah?"

So, when the Generous Lord makes a promise with emphasis, how definite, certain, and sure will it be!

4: The Meaning of Righteous Deeds:

Righteous deeds refer to actions (intended to seek Allah's pleasure) and (are done following the Book and Sunnah).

5: The Wisdom of Using Indefinite Nouns (Believer) and (Good Deed):

In the first narration, the Prophet (peace be upon him) used (a believer) and (a good deed), and both these words are indefinite nouns. Based on this, the meaning of the hadith - and Allah knows best - is:

(Indeed, Allah does not wrong (any believer) regarding (any good deed)).

Because (an indefinite noun) (provides generality). Thus, the matter of the Lord of Glory is with all believers concerning all their good deeds.

6: Explicit Mention of Receiving Provision in Return for Good Deeds:

In the second narration, the Prophet (peace be upon him) clearly informed that Allah grants the believer the reward of their good deeds in the form of provision in this world.

The same point is mentioned in the third narration by the Prophet (peace be upon him).

7: Title Written by Imam Nawawi for Two Narrations:

Imam Nawawi titled the second and third narrations as follows:

(Chapter on the Reward of the Believer for His Good Deeds in This World and the Hereafter)

8: The Worldly Reward Befitting the Generosity of Allah:

Allah, the Generous, is the One who grants in this world based on faith and righteous deeds. Obviously, faith and righteous deeds are within the capacity of the servant, and the reward given in this world is in accordance with the majesty and greatness of the Lord of Glory.

The summary of the discussion is that Allah grants the believers the reward for every good deed in this world. Additionally, He bestows upon them (a pure life), which includes pure lawful provision, happiness, contentment, worship, the ability to obey Him, an open heart for it, and in the Hereafter, the attainment of Paradise.

Therefore, those believers who desire pure lawful provision and a pleasant life should perform as many righteous deeds as possible to be among those who attain (a pure life). May Allah grant us and our generations the ability to do so. Indeed, He is All-Hearing, Responsive.

Ordering Family Members to Pray and Strictly Adhering to It Yourself

One of the causes of provision is (ordering the household to pray and firmly adhering to it yourself). By Allah's grace, the following discussion is presented under three headings:

a: Evidence

b: Three Points Regarding the Evidence

c: Four Warnings Regarding the Evidence

a: Evidence:

Allah, the Most Gracious, said:

"And enjoin prayer upon your family [and people] and be steadfast in it. We ask you not for provision; We provide for you. And the [best] outcome is for [those of] righteousness."

In this noble verse, Allah commands the Prophet (peace be upon him) to order his family members to establish prayer and to firmly adhere to it himself, clarifying that Allah does not ask for provision from them but is responsible for their sustenance.

b: Three Points Regarding the Evidence:

1: The Prophet's (peace be upon him) Practice of Acting on the Verse:

The Prophet (peace be upon him) would instruct his household to pray during times of hardship and would recite this verse. The Imams Abu Ubayd, Sa'id ibn Mansur, Ibn Mundhir, Tabari, Abu Nu'aym, and

Bayhaqi have narrated from Abdullah ibn Salam (may Allah be pleased with him) that he said:

"When a hardship or difficulty befell the household of the Prophet (peace be upon him), he would command them to pray and would recite {And enjoin prayer upon your family}."

2: Bakr al-Muzani's Practice in Accordance with the Verse and Sunnah:

Hafiz Ibn Jawzi writes in his commentary on this verse:

"When Bakr ibn Abdullah al-Muzani faced hardship in his household, he would say, 'Stand up and pray.' Then he would say, 'This is what Allah and His Messenger (peace be upon him) have commanded,' and he would recite this verse."

3: Example from Hasan al-Basri and Abu Turab:

In the same context, Hasan al-Basri stated that whenever he faced hardship, he would recite this verse and order his family to pray.

c: Four Warnings Regarding the Evidence:

1: The importance of the command and adhering to it:

The verse emphasizes the significance of not only commanding the family to pray but also being steadfast in it, highlighting a crucial aspect of leading by example in religious duties.

2: The assurance of provision from Allah:

Allah assures that He does not ask for sustenance but provides it, reinforcing the idea that reliance on Allah and fulfilling religious obligations go hand in hand.

3: The promise of a good outcome for the righteous:

The verse concludes with a promise that the best outcome is for those who are righteous, providing spiritual motivation for adhering to the command of prayer.

4: Practical implementation and its impact on the family:

Implementing this command brings about a spiritual and practical discipline within the family, leading to both worldly and spiritual benefits.

Statements of Five Commentators Regarding the Noble Verse:

Multiple commentators have regarded (ordering prayer and firmly adhering to it) as a cause for provision in light of the above verse. Here are statements from five commentators:

1: Hafiz Ibn Kathir writes:

"{We ask you not for provision; We provide for you} means when you establish prayer, provision will come to you from where you do not even imagine."

2: Sheikh Shinqiti writes:

"And He also promised provision to those who order their family to pray and are steadfast in it, as stated in His words: {And enjoin prayer upon your family and be steadfast in it}."

3: Imam Al-Qurtubi writes:

"{And enjoin prayer upon your family and be steadfast in it} is a command to consistently establish prayer as a means of ensuring provision from Allah."

4: Imam Al-Razi comments:

"The command to order family members to pray and to be steadfast in it comes with the assurance that Allah will provide for them, negating the need to worry about sustenance."

5: Imam Al-Baghawi explains:

"This verse indicates that by establishing prayer and commanding it within the household, one secures Allah's provision, making it a means to alleviate worries about sustenance."

These statements collectively highlight that commanding prayer and steadfastly adhering to it is a cause for receiving provision from Allah in ways that are beyond one's imagination. It is a testament to the spiritual and practical benefits of fulfilling this important religious obligation.

Bakar al-Muzani's Practice and the Verse's Interpretation:

According to Hafiz Ibn Jawzi in the commentary of this verse:

"When Bakar ibn Abdullah al-Muzanī's household faced poverty, he would say, 'Get up and pray.' Then he would say, 'This is what Allah and His Messenger (peace be upon him) commanded.' And he would recite this verse."

1. The General Applicability of the Verse:

Although the address in the verse is specifically to the Prophet Muhammad (peace be upon him), its general ruling applies to the entire Ummah. Allama Ibn Atiyyah wrote:

"This address is to the Prophet (peace be upon him), but its generality includes all of his Ummah."

2. Understanding of Adhering to Prayer:

According to Allama al-Wasi, the concept of being steadfast or adhering to prayer does not mean to be engaged in prayer all day and night but rather to perform prayers consistently at their appointed times.

3. No Allowance for Abandoning Effort for Livelihood:

The verse does not allow for neglecting the effort required for earning a livelihood. Allama Razi wrote:

"Understand that there is no allowance in this verse for abandoning the effort to earn a living because Allah described the qualities of the pious as: {Men whom neither trade nor sale distracts from the remembrance of Allah}."

Summary of the Discussion:

Interpretation of the Verse:

1. Allama Razi's View:

Allama Razi's intention is that the verse presented by them indicates that pious people are involved in trade and commerce, and Allah knows best.

2. Understanding the Verse in Context:

The verse {And enjoin your family to pray...} implies that one should not use the busyness of earning a livelihood as an excuse to neglect prayer. Since Allah is the provider of sustenance, it would be contradictory for Him to withhold sustenance from those who perform prayers regularly. Rather, He will open the doors of provision for those who establish prayer diligently.

If there is a conflict between performing obligatory prayers and earning a livelihood, Allah does not permit abandoning prayer for the sake of earning. Prayer must still be performed, as the one who provides sustenance is the same Allah to whom the prayers are made.

Conclusion:

The discussion emphasizes that those seeking sustenance should instruct their family members to establish prayer and adhere to it diligently themselves. Through this blessed practice, Allah will make their efforts in earning a livelihood fruitful and will provide them with sustenance from sources they cannot even imagine.

Supplication:

O Allah, grant us and our generations the ability to continue this blessed practice until death. Indeed, You are near and responsive.

Mention of "Subhan Allah wa bihamdi"

One of the causes of sustenance is mentioning "Subhan Allah wa bihamdi." Here are details under the following two headings:

1. Evidence:

Imams Ahmad and Bukhari have narrated from Abdullah bin Amr bin al-As (may Allah be pleased with him) that the Prophet Muhammad (peace be upon him) said:

"When the time of death approached Prophet Noah (peace be upon him), he said to his son:

'Indeed, I am giving you advice: I command you with two things and forbid you from two things:

I command you with:

'La ilaha illallah' (There is no deity but Allah) and

'Subhan Allah wa bihamdi' (Glory be to Allah and praise Him), for these are the prayers of everything, and with them, the creation is provided sustenance.

And I forbid you from shirk (associating partners with Allah) and pride.'"

This hadith clearly indicates that Prophet Noah (peace be upon him) informed his son that sustenance is provided with "Subhan Allah wa bihamdi."

2. Sheikh Albani's Statement:

Sheikh Albani (may Allah have mercy on him) writes while discussing the benefits of the hadith:

"The virtue of saying 'La ilaha illallah' and 'Subhan Allah wa bihamdi,' and indeed, 'Subhan Allah wa bihamdi' is a cause of sustenance for the creation."

Those seeking sustenance should frequently utter "Subhan Allah wa bihamdi," so that the Lord of Glory opens doors of provision for them. And indeed, this is not difficult for Allah.

Marriage

[Supplication and Marriage]

Among the reasons that lead to the descent of Allah's provision is supplication, which is a great means of attracting sustenance.

Likewise, marriage, as Allah Almighty said: {And marry those among you who are single and the righteous among your male slaves and female slaves. If they are poor, Allah will enrich them out of His bounty} [An-Nur: 32], and the Prophet, peace and blessings be upon him, said: (It is a right upon Allah to help those who seek marriage to remain chaste from what Allah has forbidden) or as he said, and his saying: (Three have a right upon Allah to help them: and he mentioned the one who seeks marriage to remain chaste).

Marriage is one of the means of sustenance. Please see the following two headings for a bit of detail:

A: Seven Reasons

B: Four Points Regarding These Reasons

A: Seven Reasons:

1. The command of Allah, the Exalted:

"And marry those among you who are single and the righteous among your male slaves and female slaves. If they are poor, Allah will enrich them out of His bounty. Allah is all-encompassing, all-knowing."

2. The scholars Ahmad, Tirmidhi, Nasa'i, Ibn Majah, Abu Ya'la, Ibn Hibban, Hakim, Bayhaqi, and Baghawi narrated from Abu Hurairah,

may Allah be pleased with him, that the Prophet, peace be upon him, said: "Three people have a right to the help of Allah:

- The one who fights in the cause of Allah,

- The one who marries to stay chaste,

- The slave who makes a contract to buy his freedom and seeks to fulfill it."

3. Imam Hakim and Imam Bazzar narrated from Aisha, may Allah be pleased with her, that she said: "The Messenger of Allah, peace be upon him, said: 'Marry women, for they will bring you wealth.'"

4. Imam Ibn Abi Hatim narrated from Abu Bakr Siddiq, may Allah be pleased with him, that he said: "Obey Allah in what He has commanded you regarding marriage, and He will fulfill His promise to make you rich. Allah, the Exalted, said: 'If they are poor, Allah will enrich them out of His bounty.'"

5. Imam Baghawi narrated from Umar ibn Khattab, may Allah be pleased with him, that he said: "I am amazed at the one who seeks wealth through means other than marriage, while Allah, the Exalted, says: 'If they are poor, Allah will enrich them out of His bounty.'"

6. Imam Ibn Jarir al-Tabari narrated from Ibn Abbas, may Allah be pleased with them both, that he said:

'Allah, the Exalted, commanded marriage and encouraged them (i.e., the Muslims) to do so. He commanded them to marry off their free people and slaves, and promised them wealth in that, saying:

'If they are poor, Allah will enrich them from His bounty.'

(Allah, the Exalted, commanded marriage and encouraged them (i.e., the Muslims) to do so. He commanded them to marry off their free people and slaves and promised them wealth in doing so, saying: 'If they are poor, Allah will enrich them from His bounty.')

7. Imam Ibn Jarir al-Tabari narrated from Abdullah ibn Masud, may Allah be pleased with him, that he said:

'Seek wealth through marriage. Allah, the Exalted, says:

'If they are poor, Allah will enrich them from His bounty.'

B: Four Points Regarding These Reasons:

From the aforementioned texts and narrations, it is clear that assisting the poor who marry to avoid haram (forbidden acts) is a responsibility taken on by Allah, the Provider. He has also given the glad tidings in this regard. The Prophet, peace be upon him, has conveyed the glad tidings that brides bring wealth into newly formed families by Allah's will. The companions, Abu Bakr, Umar, Ibn Abbas, and Ibn Masud, may Allah be pleased with them, strongly encouraged and urged the Ummah to marry, holding onto this great hopeful promise. To further clarify and thoroughly understand this matter, here are four points with the help of Allah:

1. The interpretation of the noble verse by eight commentators:

i. Imam Tabari wrote:

"He says: If those you marry among your single men and women and your slaves and maidservants are in need and poverty, then Allah will enrich them from His bounty. So do not let their poverty prevent you from marrying them. The scholars of interpretation have said likewise regarding what we have mentioned."

(He says: 'If those you marry among your single men and women and your slaves and maidservants are in need and poverty, then surely Allah will enrich them from His bounty. Do not let their poverty prevent you from marrying them.' The scholars of interpretation have said likewise regarding what we have mentioned.)

ii. Hafiz Ibn al-Jawzi wrote:

Allah, the Exalted, said regarding the free people:

'If they are poor, Allah will enrich them from His bounty.'

He then explains:

"He informed them that marriage is a means of eliminating poverty."

iii. Allama Qurtubi wrote that Allah, the Exalted, said regarding the free people:

"Do not abstain from marrying because of the poverty of the man or the woman. If they are poor, Allah will enrich them from His bounty."

This is a promise of wealth for those who marry seeking Allah's pleasure and to avoid His prohibitions.

iv: Hafiz Ibn Kathir wrote:

"Regarding the well-known generosity and kindness of Allah, the Exalted, it is well known that He grants sustenance sufficient for both the one who marries and his wife."

v: Allama Suyuti wrote:

"There is encouragement for marriage in this verse, and indeed it brings sustenance."

vi: Allama Alusi wrote:

"It is evident that this is indeed a promise from Allah, the Exalted, to enrich."

vii: Sheikh Muhammad Amin Shanqiti wrote:

"The statement of Allah, the Exalted, in this noble verse: {If they are poor, Allah will enrich them from His bounty} includes a promise from Allah to enrich the poor who marry from the free people and slaves, and Allah does not break His promise."

viii: Sheikh Abu Bakr Jazairi, while mentioning the guidance derived from the verse, wrote:

"Allah's promise to enrich the poor who marry."

2: Titles written on the hadith (Thalathun kulluhum... etc.):

Regarding the hadith mentioned under number 2, the titles written by three scholars are as follows:

i: Imam Tirmidhi wrote:

"Chapter on what has been mentioned about the Mujahid, the Mukatib, and the one who marries, and Allah's help for these three."

II: IMAM NASA'I WROTE:

"Chapter on Allah's help for the one who marries seeking chastity."

iii: Imam Ibn Hibban wrote:

"Mention of Allah, the Exalted's, help for the one who intends chastity in marriage and the one who intends to pay off in his contract."

3: Title written on the hadith (Tazawwajun nisaa...):

Hafiz Haythami wrote:

"Chapter: Marry women, they will bring you wealth."

4: Three Warnings:

i: The promise of wealth due to marriage is for the one who marries seeking, by their marriage, to obey Allah, lower their gaze, and protect their chastity. Here are the statements of two commentators in this regard:

"Indeed, the one who is promised wealth through marriage is the one who seeks, through marriage, to assist in obeying Allah by lowering the gaze and protecting the private parts, as explained by the Prophet, peace be upon him, in the authentic hadith: 'O youth...'"

"It is evident that the promise of wealth made by Allah to the one who marries is indeed for the one who marries with the intention of lowering the gaze, protecting the private parts, and aiding in obeying Allah, as explained by the Prophet (peace be upon him) in the authentic hadith: 'O youth...' to the end of the hadith.

This is good news for those poor Muslims who wish to marry to protect their faith but lack financial resources. If they marry with the sincere intention of protecting their faith and following the Sunnah of the Messenger of Allah (peace be upon him), Allah will grant them financial wealth as well."

B: The meaning of Allah making someone wealthy upon marriage does not imply that the one who marries should not strive for sustenance or abandon their previous efforts. Rather, it means that Allah, the Exalted, will grant them the ability to adopt such ways and means of acquiring sustenance that the maintenance of the family formed by marriage will not be a problem for them. Sheikh Ibn Ashur writes:

"Allah making them wealthy means that He will grant them the ability to adopt such means in daily life that their economic efforts will be successful and their trade profitable. The verse implies that Allah has taken the responsibility of covering the additional expenses arising from marriage."

The conclusion is that unmarried people should marry, despite their poverty, with the intention of obeying Allah and avoiding what is forbidden. They should keep their marriage as simple as possible, completely avoiding extravagance and wastefulness. They should strive hard for lawful sustenance and correct any deficiencies in this effort. If they do this, by Allah's grace, the doors of sustenance will be opened for them.

Leaving Early in the Morning

One of the means of obtaining sustenance is to start early in the morning. The details regarding this are provided under the following three headings:

A: The First Proof and Five Related Points

B: The Second Proof and One Related Point

C: A Warning

A: The First Proof and Five Related Points

(i) Proof:

Imams Abu Dawood Tayalisi, Saeed bin Mansoor, Ahmad, Abu Dawood, Tirmidhi, Nasa'i, Ibn Majah, Darimi, and Ibn Hibban have narrated from Hazrat Sakhr Ghamidi (may Allah be pleased with him) that the Prophet (peace be upon him) said in a supplication:

"O Allah, bless my nation in their early mornings."

"And when he sent out a military expedition or an army, he sent it in the early morning."

"Sakhr (may Allah be pleased with him) was a merchant, and he used to send out his trade caravans in the early morning, so he became wealthy, and his wealth increased."

(ii) Five Points Related to the Proof:

1: Explanation of the Hadith:

Mulla Ali Qari writes:

"(Bukooriha) means to leave early in the morning, and this includes going out in search of knowledge, seeking sustenance, and traveling, etc."

2: The Significance of This Supplication:

The Prophet (peace be upon him) prayed to Allah to bless the early mornings of those in his nation who start their work early. The significance of this supplication is immense! The one making the supplication is the beloved and friend of Allah, whose supplications are the most accepted among all creatures! Peace and blessings of my Lord be upon him.

And the supplication for (Barakah) means that the divine goodness remains and endures in it and that (there is no reproach in using it in the Hereafter.)

3: Encouragement Through the Prophet's Own Practice:

The Prophet (peace be upon him) did not only pray but also demonstrated the importance and significance of starting work early through his own practice by sending out military detachments and armies early in the morning.

4: The Narrator's Application of the Hadith and Attaining Blessings:

The fortunate narrator of the hadith, Hazrat Sakhr Ghamidi (may Allah be pleased with him), heard, understood, and conveyed the encouragement of the Prophet (peace be upon him) and also acted upon it himself. Consequently, Allah made him wealthy and prosperous in this world. The words in the Musnad's narration are:

"His wealth increased so much that he did not know where to put his wealth (i.e., how to spend it)."

In Tuhfatul Ahwadhi, it is mentioned:

"(Fathri) means he became wealthy due to following the Sunnah and the acceptance of the Prophet's (peace be upon him) supplication."

This was the immediate worldly reward for following the Sunnah. The reward in the Hereafter will be even greater!

The Command of Allah Almighty:

{And the abode of the Hereafter is better and an excellent abode for the pious}

5: Titles of Five Hadith Scholars on the Hadith:

To increase the desire for the blessings described in the Hadith, the titles written by five Hadith scholars on this subject are as follows:

a. Imam Tirmidhi writes: (Chapter on What Has Been Reported About Early Morning Trade)

b. Imam Ibn Majah writes: (Chapter on the Expected Blessings in Going Out Early)

c. Imam Darimi has written: (Chapter on "Bless My Ummah in Their Early Mornings")

d. Imam Ibn Hibban has written: (Mention of What is Recommended for a Person to Start War and Other Matters in the Early Mornings to Seek Blessings from the Prayer of the Chosen One)

e. Hafiz Mundhiri has written: (Encouragement for Going Out Early in the Morning to Seek Sustenance and Other Matters)

5: Note:

A major obstacle to going out early in the morning for seeking sustenance and other tasks is not getting enough sleep at night. The best way to address this issue is to follow the Sunnah by going to bed early.

Avoid wasting time on trivial and meaningless activities that prevent you from sleeping early. Move useful and necessary nighttime tasks and activities to the daytime as much as possible. Serious and consistent efforts in this regard can be expected to yield good results from Allah Almighty.

Truthfulness in Trade and Declaring the Defects of Goods

One of the means of earning sustenance is being truthful in transactions and declaring the defects of the goods presented. With divine grace, the discussion on this subject is provided under the following two headings:

a. Evidence

b. Five Points Regarding the Evidence

a. Evidence:

Imam Bukhari and Imam Muslim have reported from Hazrat Hakim bin Hizam that the Prophet Muhammad said:

"The two traders have the option to cancel the sale as long as they have not separated. If they speak the truth and clarify the defects, their trade will be blessed. But if they lie and conceal the defects, the blessing of their trade will be removed."

b. Five Points Regarding the Evidence:

The Prophet Muhammad clearly stated in this Hadith that the truthfulness of those engaged in trade and their declaration of the defects of the goods will bring blessings to their trade. In this regard, consider the following five points:

1. Explanation of the Hadith:

Allama Qurtubi writes in the explanation of the Hadith:

"If both the buyer and the seller are truthful about the price and the condition of the goods, and they clarify the defects, blessings will be granted in terms of increasing the price and providing lasting benefit from the goods."

2. A Title Written on the Hadith:

Imam Ibn Hibban has written the following title on this:

(Mention of the Command for Both Traders to Adhere to Truthfulness in Their Transactions and to Declare Any Known Defects, as This Causes Blessings in Their Trade)

3. Gaining Worldly Benefits from the Hereafter:

(i) Allama Ibn Abi Jamrah writes:

"This indicates that worldly gains come from the Hereafter. The reason for this is that blessings come from truthfulness, which is an attribute of the Hereafter. Truth-telling is rewarded and is among the most complete traits of faith. Scholars have said:

'Whoever speaks the truth and confirms it, will surely get closer to his goal.'"

The Prophet Muhammad expressed this in the words:

"What is with Allah cannot be attained except through obedience to Allah."

(ii) Hafiz Ibn Hajar, while describing the benefits of the Hadith, wrote:

"And that the actions of the Hereafter lead to the goodness of both this world and the Hereafter."

4. The Means of Wealth for Abdul Rahman bin Auf:

When Hazrat Abdul Rahman bin Auf was asked about the reasons for his wealth, he responded:

"I have never lied, nor practiced deceit, nor sold on credit, nor refused any profit, however small it may be."

5: Wathilah's Care in Declaring the Defects of His Goods:

Imams Ahmad, Hakim, and Bayhaqi have reported from Abu Siba' who narrated:

"I bought a she-camel from Wathilah bin Asqa' at his home. When I was leaving with it, Wathilah bin Asqa' followed us, dragging his cloak."

He said: "O servant of Allah! Have you bought this she-camel?"

I said: "Yes."

He asked: "Has its defect been disclosed to you?"

I replied: "What defect? It is a fat, apparently healthy she-camel."

He said: "Do you intend to travel on it or do you intend to use it for meat?"

I said: "Rather, I intend to perform Hajj on it."

He said: "Indeed, there is a defect in its hoof."

The narrator said: "He (the buyer) said: 'May Allah set you right! What do you want with this? Are you ruining my transaction?'"

He replied: "I heard the Messenger of Allah saying: 'It is not lawful for anyone selling something to withhold its defects, nor is it lawful for someone who knows the defect to conceal it.'"

Allah is Great! How diligent Wathilah was in declaring the defect of his own goods! May Allah be pleased with him and grant him peace.

The essence of this discussion is that being truthful in transactions and clarifying the defects of goods, rather than concealing them, brings blessings from Allah in trade.

Those desiring blessings in sustenance should make honesty and declaring defects in their transactions a principle and practice of their lives. May Allah grant us the ability to do so. Ameen, O Ever-Living, O Sustainer.

Measuring Grain

One of the means of sustenance is (measuring grain during transactions). A detailed discussion on this topic is presented under the following two headings:

a. Four Narrations

b. Seven Points Regarding These Narrations

a. Four Narrations:

1. Imam Bukhari narrated from Miqdad bin Ma'dikarib, who reported that the Prophet said:

"Measure your grain, and you will be blessed."

2. Imam Ibn Majah narrated from Abdullah bin Busr Mazni, who reported that he heard the Prophet say:

"Measure your grain, and you will be blessed in it."

3. Imam Ibn Majah also narrated from Abu Ayyub, who reported that the Prophet said:

"Measure your grain, and you will be blessed in it."

4. Imam Ibn al-Najjar narrated from Ali, who said:

"Measure your grain, for there is a blessing in measured grain."

b. Seven Points Regarding These Narrations:

1. The Purpose of Measuring Grain:

The purpose is to ascertain its quantity.

Allama Mazhar states:

"The purpose of measuring grain is to know the amount that a person borrows, sells, and buys."

Allama Aini writes: "The wisdom in measuring is that through it, the amount of grain kept and prepared for consumption is known."

2. Wisdom of Measuring During Transactions:

Both the seller and the buyer are obligated to measure the grain during transactions to avoid ambiguity and ensure justice.

Allama Mazhar writes after his aforementioned statement:

"If it is not measured, the sold and bought items will be unknown, and that is not permissible."

Similarly, Allama Tayyibi writes:

"Measuring during sale and purchase is commanded to establish justice and fairness."

Allama Manawi has written:

"As for in selling and buying, it is obvious."

3. Ensuring Justice in Transactions:

By measuring, both parties can ensure fairness and avoid disputes over quantity.

4. Avoiding Deception:

Measuring prevents deception and cheating in the quantity of goods exchanged.

5. Encouraging Trust:

When both parties adhere to the practice of measuring, it fosters trust and reliability in business dealings.

6. Divine Blessings:

Following this practice invites blessings from Allah in one's sustenance and trade.

7. Setting a Standard:

Measuring sets a standard procedure that others in the community can follow, promoting a culture of fairness and honesty.

By adhering to the practice of measuring grain during transactions, one invites divine blessings and ensures fairness and transparency in trade. Those seeking blessings in their sustenance should adopt honesty and clarity in their transactions as a way of life. May Allah grant us the ability to do so. Amen, O Ever-Living, O Sustainer.

(It is evident to measure during transactions.)

Imam Ibn Hibban titled this hadith as follows:

Mentioning the command for the buyer to measure grain in expectation of blessings

3. Wisdom of Measuring for Personal Use:

Allama Mazhar wrote about measuring grain when taking out or storing it for one's family:

"Similarly, if one does not measure the grain for his family, it might sometimes be less than their need, causing harm to them, or sometimes more than their need, and he would not know how much to store for the whole year. The Prophet commanded measuring so that people have knowledge and certainty about what they are doing."

Allama Manawi wrote similarly:

"As for measuring grain for the family, it is because if it is taken out without measuring, it might sometimes be less than needed, causing harm, or sometimes more, and the person would not know how much to store for the entire year. The Prophet commanded measuring so that the grain remains for the desired duration."

4. Questions and Comments on Three Hadiths about Measuring Grain for Use:

Questions have been raised about measuring grain given for use, based on three hadiths. Here are those hadiths and comments on them:

a. Imam Bukhari narrated from Aisha that she said:

"When the Prophet passed away, there was nothing in my pantry but a small amount of barley. I kept eating from it for a long time until I measured it, and it was gone."

Allama Muhammad Anwar Shah Kashmiri believes that the command (measure your grain) applies when storing grain for food, but once the grain is in the house and being used, measuring the remaining grain in the vessel might remove the blessing, as indicated in Aisha's hadith.

Hafiz Ibn Hajar believes that the command to measure grain applies during transactions, as it concerns the rights of the seller and buyer. As for measuring while using it, this might sometimes lead to stinginess; hence, it is disliked to measure grain when giving it for consumption.

b. Imam Bukhari narrated from Asma that she said:

"I said, 'O Messenger of Allah, I have nothing but the wealth that Zubair (my husband) gives me. Can I give it in charity?' The Prophet said, 'Give in charity, and do not hoard, lest it is withheld from you.'"

In another narration, it says: Spend, and do not count, lest Allah counts for you; and do not hoard, lest Allah withholds from you.

(Spend in the way of Allah, do not count, so that it is not counted against you, and do not hoard, so that Allah does not withhold from you.)

In both narrations, the Prophet forbade hoarding and counting.

- Hoarding: Tying the edge of the container with a strap.

- Counting: Measuring or counting the quantity of something.

The purpose of these narrations was not to prohibit Asma from measuring grain, but to prevent her from not giving charity out of fear of depletion. Hafiz Ibn Hajar wrote:

"The meaning is to prohibit withholding charity out of fear of depletion."

Hafiz Ibn Hajar also wrote elsewhere:

"The meaning is not to gather in the container and be stingy in spending, or you will be rewarded in kind."

c. Imam Bayhaqi narrated from Abu Huraira that the Prophet said:

"O Bilal, spend, and do not fear poverty from the One who is on the Throne."

Allama Tayyibi, referring to this hadith, wrote:

"And when spending, counting and calculating is prohibited."

Using this hadith to argue against measuring grain for personal use does not seem weighty—Allah knows best. The prohibited act appears to be being stingy and withholding spending.

Allama Aini wrote about measuring grain for use:

"And the Prophet would store a year's worth of food for his family, and this was only after knowing the quantity by measuring."

5. Titles Given by Hadith Scholars:

The titles given by three hadith scholars on the mentioned hadiths are as follows:

a. Imam Bukhari wrote:

Chapter: What is recommended about measuring grain

b. Imam Ibn Majah wrote:

Chapter: The hope of blessings in measuring grain

c. Imam Bayhaqi wrote:

Chapter: The narrations about seeking blessings by measuring grain

Note:

In all three titles, the blessings obtained by measuring grain are not limited to buying and selling.

6. Meaning of Blessing:

Allama Manawi wrote:

"It means there is good, blessing, and growth in it."

7. Intention of Following the Sunnah When Measuring:

While measuring grain, the intention should be to follow the Prophet's sunnah. Allama Mazhar stated:

"Whoever observes the Sunnah of the Prophet will find great blessings in this world and great reward in the hereafter."

Hafiz Ibn Hajar wrote that the blessing in measuring grain comes from complying with the Prophet's command, and when this command is neglected, the blessing is taken away due to the misfortune of disobedience. Hafiz Ibn Hajar further stated that the blessing does not come only from measuring but from the intention to comply with the command of measuring.

In summary, those seeking blessings in grain should measure it during buying, selling, and using, following the Sunnah of the Prophet. O Generous Lord, grant us the ability to do so. Indeed, You are near and responsive.

The Sincere Intention to Repay a Debt

Among the means of livelihood is a true, sincere, and determined intention to repay debts. The details under the following three headings illustrate this:

A. Three Hadiths:

1. Imam Ahmad narrated from Aisha, who reported that the Messenger of Allah said:

"No servant has a sincere intention to repay a debt except that Allah, the Exalted, helps him."

Another narration states:

"He has help and protection from Allah."

And in a narration by Tabarani:

"He has help from Allah and it becomes a cause for his provision."

2. Imam Bukhari narrated from Abu Huraira that the Prophet said:

"Whoever takes the wealth of people intending to repay it, Allah will repay it on his behalf."

Hafiz Ibn Hajar, in explaining this hadith, wrote:

"It encourages the correctness of the intention to repay a debt and warns against its corruption."

3. In a hadith narrated by Imam Ibn Majah from Maimuna, she reported that she heard the Prophet say:

"No Muslim takes a loan, intending to repay it, except that Allah repays it on his behalf in this world."

B. Four Benefits of a Sincere and Determined Intention to Repay Debt:

From the above hadiths, the following blessings of a sincere and firm intention to repay a debt are evident:

1. Allah's help and assistance for the debtor.

2. The appointment of a protector for him.

3. The provision of means for his sustenance.

4. Repayment of his debt.

C. A Story Illustrating the Blessings of a Sincere Intention to Repay Debt:

Imam Bukhari narrated from Abdullah bin Zubair, who reported:

"When Zubair stood on the day of the Battle of the Camel, he called me. I stood by his side, and he said:

'O my son, today only a wrongdoer or a wronged one will be killed. I believe I will be killed today as a wronged one. Indeed, my greatest concern is my debt. Do you think anything will remain of our wealth after repaying our debt?'

He continued:

'O my son, sell our property to repay my debt.'

He also willed a third of his wealth. At that time, he had nine sons and nine daughters."

Abdullah narrated:

"He kept advising me about his debt and said:

'O my son, if you are unable to repay it, seek help from my Master.'

I did not understand his intent, so I asked:

'O father, who is your Master?'

He replied:

'Allah.'

The intention to repay a debt sincerely and firmly brings various blessings and Allah's assistance. It is a significant cause for receiving divine help in both repaying the debt and sustaining one's livelihood.

He (Abdullah) narrated:

"By Allah! Whenever I faced a distress regarding his debt, I would say:

'O Lord of Zubair! Repay his debt.'

Then it would be repaid.

Thus, Zubair was killed (in that instance). He did not leave behind any dinars or dirhams. His inheritance was land, including the land of Ghabah, eleven houses in Madinah, two houses in Basra, one house in Kufa, and one in Egypt."

He narrated: "The background of his debt was that someone would come to him with their wealth to keep in trust, but Zubair would say, 'I will not keep it as a trust, but as a debt, because I fear it might get lost.'"

Abdullah bin Zubair narrated:

"I calculated the amount of debt he owed, and it was twenty-two million."

Hakim bin Hizam met Abdullah bin Zubair and asked:

'O nephew! How much debt does my brother owe?'

He concealed the actual amount and said, 'One hundred thousand.' Hakim said:

'By Allah! I do not think your wealth is sufficient for this.'

Abdullah said to him:

'What would you think if it were two million and two hundred thousand?'

He replied:

'I do not think you can manage this. If you are unable to repay any part of it, seek help from me.'

He (Abdullah) narrated:

'Zubair bought the land of Ghabah for one hundred and seventy thousand, and Abdullah sold it for one million and six hundred thousand.'

Then he announced:

'Whoever has a debt owed by Zubair, let him come to us at Ghabah.'

So, Abdullah bin Jaafar came, and he had four hundred thousand owed by Zubair. He said to Abdullah:

'If you wish, I will forgive this debt.' Abdullah said, 'No.'

He said, 'If you wish to delay (the payment), delay it.' Abdullah said, 'No.'

He said, 'Assign me a portion of this land.'

Abdullah said, 'From here to here is yours.'

Abdullah sold parts of the land and houses and paid off the entire debt. However, there were still four and a half shares left of Ghabah. Abdullah came to Muawiyah, where Amr bin Uthman, Mundhir bin Zubair, and Ibn Zam'ah were present.

Muawiyah asked, 'What is the price of the land in Ghabah?'

They replied, 'One hundred thousand per share.'

He asked, 'How many shares are left?'

They replied, 'Four and a half.'

Mundhir bin Zubair said, 'I take a share for one hundred thousand.'

Amr bin Uthman said, 'I take a share for one hundred thousand.'

Ibn Zam'ah said, 'I take a share for one hundred thousand.'

Muawiyah asked, 'How many are left?'

They replied, 'One and a half.'

He (Muawiyah) said, 'I take it for one hundred and fifty thousand.'

When Abdullah bin Zubair finished repaying the debt, the children of Zubair said:

'Distribute our inheritance among us now.'

He replied:

'No, by Allah! I will not distribute it among you until I announce during the Hajj season for four years:

"Listen! Whoever has a debt owed by Zubair, let him come to us, and we will repay it.'"

He (the narrator) narrated: 'He announced this every year during the Hajj season. After four years had passed, he distributed the inheritance among them.'

He narrated: 'Zubair had four wives. Abdullah took out the third part (as per the will) after repaying the debt. Each wife received twelve hundred thousand.'"

From this incident, among the multiple points observed are the following two:

1. Zubair's concern and arrangement for repaying the debt:

Three points indicating this are as follows:

In another narration, it is stated: He said:

"Look, my dear son, at my debt, for I do not leave behind anything more important to me than it."

(My dear son, sell our property and repay the debt.)

(If you become helpless regarding any aspect of it, then seek help from my Lord (i.e., Allah).)

b: The repayment of seemingly very difficult debt through sincere intention:

By keeping the following points in mind, it will be easy to envision the situation with the divine grace: If the debt amount had been only one hundred thousand, even then the property left by Zubair would not have been sufficient for its repayment. When he was informed that the debt amount was twenty-two hundred thousand, he spontaneously said: "I do not think you have the ability to repay this."

Hafiz Ibn Hajar writes:

"The reality is that the inheritance was significantly less compared to the debt, but Allah put blessings in it, by creating such a desire in the hearts of the buyers of the property he left behind, that its price increased manyfold."

The debt was repaid, and the heirs received so much wealth that each of the four wives received twelve hundred thousand as their share.

In summary, indebted people should have a sincere, strong, and firm intention to repay their debt. Allah will help and assist them, appoint protectors for their care and protection, and ensure their debt is repaid in this world. And that is not difficult for Allah.

Hafiz Ibn Hajar, in the commentary of another hadith, writes:

"In it, there is encouragement for the correct intention for the repayment of debt and a warning against its improper intention."

Entering the house with greeting

Going towards the mosque

Going out for striving in the cause of Allah

Visiting the sick

Supporting the ruler in matters of truth

Sitting at home without backbiting

Each of the aforementioned acts is among the means of sustenance. With divine guidance, the following discussion will be conducted under two headings:

A: Two Narrations

B: Two Points Regarding These Narrations

A: Two Narrations:

1. Imam Ibn Hibban narrated from Abu Umamah that indeed the Messenger of Allah said:

"Three types of people, all of whom have Allah's guarantee: If they live, they will be provided for and be sufficient, and if they die, Allah will admit them to Paradise: whoever enters his house and greets, he has Allah's guarantee,

whoever goes to the mosque, he has Allah's guarantee,

and whoever goes out in the cause of Allah, he has Allah's guarantee."

2. Imam Ibn Hibban narrated from Mu'adh bin Jabal that the Messenger of Allah said:

"Whoever strives in the cause of Allah, he has Allah's guarantee,

and whoever visits a sick person, he has Allah's guarantee,

and whoever goes to the mosque in the morning or evening, he has Allah's guarantee,

and whoever comes to a ruler to honor and support him, he has Allah's guarantee,

and whoever sits in his house without backbiting anyone, he has Allah's guarantee."

B: Two Points Regarding These Narrations:

1. From the aforementioned narrations, it is known that Allah guarantees the following eight types of people:

Imam Ibn Hibban titled the second narration as follows:

(Mention of the qualities which, if a person adopts them, Allah becomes their guarantor)

2. In the first narration, the Prophet described the worldly and otherworldly benefits and fruits of being guaranteed by Allah with the following words:

"If he lives, he will be provided for and be sufficient, and if he dies, Allah will admit him to Paradise."

Allahu Akbar! How great and blessed is Allah's guarantee!

Receiving provision from the Sustainer Lord in life and being sufficient from worries and sorrows by the Almighty and Powerful Lord!

Moreover, being admitted to Paradise by the Lord of Majesty in the afterlife!

Imam Ibn Hibban titled the first narration as follows:

(Mention of Allah's guarantee for the one who greets his family upon entering his house, for Paradise if he dies, and for sufficiency and provision if he lives)

Seekers of provision, those wishing to be free from worries, and those desiring to enter Paradise should make each of the above-mentioned eight qualities a part of their lives. O Allah, make us among them by Your mercy. Indeed, You are All-Hearing, Responsive.

Establishment of Limits

One of the means of sustenance is (establishing the limits of Allah on His earth). Detailed discussion on this topic can be seen under the following two headings:

A: Three Narrations

B: Three Points Regarding These Narrations

A: Three Narrations:

1. Imam Ibn Majah narrated from Ibn Umar that indeed the Messenger of Allah said:

"Establishing one limit from the limits of Allah is better than forty nights of rain in the cities of Allah."

2. The Imams Ahmad, Nasa'i, Ibn Majah, and Ibn Hibban narrated from Abu Hurairah, who reported: "The Messenger of Allah said:

"Establishing one limit on the earth is better for the people of the earth than being rained upon for forty mornings."

3. Imam Nasa'i narrated from Abu Hurairah, who said:

"Establishing one limit on a land is better for its people than forty nights of rain."

Although this is a saying of Abu Hurairah, it is as if it is the statement of the Prophet because the companions would not say such things on their own. Such sayings are called (Marfu' Hukman).

B: Three Points Regarding These Narrations:

1. The title Imam Ibn Hibban gave to the second narration:

(Mention of the command to establish limits in cities, because establishing a limit in a city is more widely beneficial than multiple times the rain if it spreads).

2. In the explanation of the second hadith, Allama Suyuti states:

"(Better for the people of the earth) means more blessed in sustenance and other things such as fruits and rivers."

3. The reason for the blessings of establishing limits:

Allama Taybi, while stating the reason for the blessings of establishing limits, writes:

"And this is because establishing them deters people from sins and disobedience, and it opens the gates of the heavens well and thoroughly. Abandoning them and neglecting them causes people to immerse in sins, which is a reason for being seized by drought, dryness, and the destruction of the people."

Rulers who desire the well-being of their subjects should establish the divine limits in their countries so that Allah opens the gates of blessings for them, removes poverty, and grants abundance and ample provision. The public should also compel their rulers in this matter and fully cooperate with them in the establishment of limits. Perhaps the nation may be saved from drought, dryness, and hardship. And this is not difficult for Allah.

Steadfastness

One of the means of sustenance is (steadfastness). Regarding this, a discussion is presented under the following two headings:

A: Evidence

B: Two Points Regarding the Evidence

A: Evidence:

Allah has said:

"And if they had remained steadfast on the (right) way, We would certainly have given them abundant water to drink."

B: Two Points Regarding the Evidence:

1. Meaning of Steadfastness:

Two scholars' statements:

1. Allama Raghib Isfahani writes:

"Steadfastness of a person is adhering to the straight path."

2. Imam Nawawi wrote: The scholars stated: "The meaning of steadfastness is adhering to the obedience of Allah."

2. Seven commentators' statements regarding the noble verse:

1. Ibn Abbas said:

Steadfastness means remaining firm on obedience and abundant pure water means a lot of pure water."

The path means the path of truth and the phrase "We would certainly have given them abundant water to drink" means that We would give them a lot of wealth."

If a human or jinn or both adhered to the Islamic community, We would increase their sustenance. The specific mention of (abundant water) is because it is the basis of livelihood, and its abundance is the foundation of ample sustenance.

The statement of Allah "We would certainly have given them abundant water to drink" (is a promise of good reward in this world for steadfastness in religion), a sign of Allah's pleasure, and a glad tiding of reward in the hereafter."

The first truth is that there is a connection between steadfastness on the unique path leading to Allah and a prosperous life for nations and communities. This connection is still a proven fact. Arabs lived a life of hardship in the desert, but when they remained steadfast on the path of truth, they were given abundant water and lands with ample sustenance. Then when they deviated from the path of truth, they were deprived of prosperity.

"Allah's conditional promise is for all people and for every time and place."

In summary, if people steadfastly adhere to the path of truth in every aspect and corner of life: beliefs, worship, dealings, ethics, social, communal, economic, political, individual, communal, and in all kinds of situations: joy and sorrow, strength and weakness, health and illness, wealth and poverty, dominance and subjugation, travel and residence, peace and war, in all conditions if they remain firm on the Shariah of the Lord of the worlds, then Allah will grant them abundance, prosperity, and ample sustenance in this world. This promise of the All-Powerful Lord is for all people, no matter the time they live in or the place they reside. This promise is for individuals as well as for nations and communities.

Therefore, whoever seeks abundance in sustenance should adhere to the Shariah of the Sustainer with steadfastness and perseverance. May Allah include us, our brothers and sisters, families, and generations among such fortunate people. Indeed, He is the All-Hearing, the Responsive.

Proven Supplications for Seeking Sustenance

Allah, the Generous, has given His servants a powerful weapon in the form of prayer to fulfill their needs and protect them from undesirable things. Seekers of sustenance should make full use of this weapon. The righteous have always benefited from it. Numerous supplications related to seeking sustenance are established from the Prophet Muhammad (peace be upon him). By divine grace, many supplications from the Quran and Sunnah are mentioned below:

A: Prayer of Prophet Ibrahim (peace be upon him) for his offspring's sustenance:

Allah, the Generous, mentioned that Prophet Ibrahim (peace be upon him) prayed for his offspring:

"Then incline the hearts of the people toward them and provide them with fruits so that they may be grateful."

Two Notes:

1. Allah accepted this plea from His friend Ibrahim (peace be upon him). Regarding the effect of this prayer, Allah said:

"Have We not made the sacred house a place of security, to which fruits of all kinds are brought?"

2. Prophet Ibrahim (peace be upon him) began his plea with "Our Lord." One who starts the supplication for sustenance with this sentence should add "Our Lord" at the beginning and omit "Then" to connect with the previous sentence, as follows:

{رَّبَّنَا إِجْعَلْ أَفْئِدَةً مِّنَ النَّاسِ تَهْوِى ٓ إِلَيْهِمْ

وَارْزُقْهُم مِّنَ الثَّمَرَٰتِ لَعَلَّهُمْ يَشْكُرُونَ}

"OUR LORD, INCLINE THE hearts of the people toward them and provide them with fruits so that they may be grateful."

And Allah knows best.

B: The Prayer of Prophet Musa (peace be upon him):

Prophet Musa (peace be upon him), fleeing from Pharaoh's oppression, reached Midian in a state of helplessness. Upon seeing two girls with their flock of sheep at a well, he asked about their situation. After watering their sheep, he sat under a tree and prayed to Allah with the following words:

{رَبِّ إِنِّى لِمَآ أَنزَلْتَ إِلَىَّ مِنْ خَيْرٍ فَقِيرٌ}

"MY LORD, INDEED I AM in need of whatever good You send down to me."

Dr. Muhammad Luqman Salafi wrote in his commentary: Musa (peace be upon him) watered the girls' sheep, then prayed under a tree, stating that he was in need of the means of sustenance before him, which was the need for a laborer by the father of the two girls and his own need for sustenance.

Allah heard Prophet Musa's plea. Not only was labor provided but also a wife was given. Allah Himself said:

"Then one of the two women came to him walking with shyness. She said: 'Indeed, my father invites you that he may reward you for having watered our sheep.' So when he came to him and related the story, he said: 'Fear not. You have escaped from the people who do wrong.' One of the two women said: 'O my father, hire him. Indeed, the best one you can hire is the strong, the trustworthy.' He said: 'I wish to marry one of these two daughters of mine to you on the condition that you serve me for eight years. But if you complete ten years, it will be from you. And I do not wish to put you in hardship. You will find me, if Allah wills, among the righteous.' He said: 'That is between me and you. Whichever of the two terms I complete, there will be no injustice to me, and Allah is Surety over what we say.'"

Those struggling for employment and sustenance should adopt Prophet Musa's prayer. The same Allah who granted Prophet Musa sustenance and a wife without bribery or recommendations in a state of helplessness can still provide all these blessings.

"That is the tradition of Allah which has already passed before. And you will not find in the tradition of Allah any change."

C: The Prayer of Prophet Isa (peace be upon him):

Prophet Isa (peace be upon him) prayed upon his people's request, as Allah mentioned:

"And provide us with sustenance, and You are the best of providers."

Allah accepted his prayer and said:

"Allah said: 'Indeed, I am sending it down to you.'"

Note:

One who prays for sustenance with the aforementioned supplication should begin with "Our Lord" and then say:

((رَبَّنَا) ارْزُقْنَا وَأَنْتَ خَيْرُ الرَّازِقِينَ) ـ

"OUR LORD, PROVIDE US with sustenance, and You are the best of providers."

And Allah knows best.

D: The Prophet Muhammad's (peace be upon him) prayers for sustenance:

Several prescribed supplications for sustenance are recorded. Among them are five as follows:

اَللّٰهُمَّ أَصْلِحْ لِي دِينِي الَّذِي هُوَ عِصْمَةُ أَمْرِي،

وَأَصْلِحْ لِي دُنْيَاىَ الَّتِي فِيهَا مَعَاشِي،

وَأَصْلِحْ لِي آخِرَتِي الَّتِي فِيهَا مَعَادِي،

وَاجْعَلِ الْحَيَاةَ زِيَادَةً لِّي فِي كُلِّ خَيْرٍ،

وَاجْعَلِ الْمَوْتَ رَاحَةً لِّي مِنْ كُلِّ شَرٍّ۔"

"O ALLAH! SET RIGHT for me my religion, which is the safeguard of my affairs; and set right for me my worldly affairs, in which is my livelihood; and set right for me my hereafter, in which is my return; and make life an increase for me in every good; and make death a relief for me from every evil."

Regarding this prayer, Allama Qurtubi wrote:

"This great supplication encompasses the goodness of both this world and the hereafter, as well as religion and worldly matters. Every listener should memorize it and recite it during the times of night and day, hoping that during the time of acceptance, this prayer may be answered, leading to the goodness of this world and the hereafter."

It is narrated from Anas that he said:

The Prophet (peace be upon him) used to say:

"اَللّٰهُمَّ إِنِّيْ أَسْأَلُكَ الْهُدَىٰ، وَالتُّقَىٰ، وَالْعَفَافَ، وَالْغِنَىٰ،

"O ALLAH, I ASK YOU for guidance, piety, chastity, and affluence."

The Prophet (peace be upon him) would say:

"اَللّٰهُمَّ إِنِّيْ أَسْأَلُكَ عِلْمًا نَافِعًا، وَعَمَلًا مُتَقَبَّلًا، وَرِزْقًا طَيِّبًا."

"O ALLAH, I ASK YOU for beneficial knowledge, accepted deeds, and pure sustenance."

The Messenger of Allah (peace be upon him) used to say:

"اَللّٰهُمَّ اجْعَلْ أَوْسَعَ رِزْقِكَ عَلَيَّ عِنْدَ كِبَرِ سِنِّيْ وَانْقِطَاعِ عُمُرِيْ."

"O ALLAH, GRANT ME THE widest sustenance at the time of my old age and the end of my life."

A person said: "O Messenger of Allah (peace be upon him), Anas, your servant, ask Allah for him."

The Prophet (peace be upon him) said:

"O Allah, increase his wealth and offspring, and bless him in what You have given him."

Note:

This supplication should be recited for oneself as follows:

اَللّٰهُمَّ أَكْثِرْ مَالِي وَوَلَدِي، وَبَارِكْ لِي فِيمَا أَعْطَيْتَنِي

"O ALLAH, INCREASE MY wealth and offspring, and bless me in what You have given me."

Acceptance of the Prophet's (peace be upon him) supplication:

Allah, the Generous, accepted the Prophet's (peace be upon him) supplication. Imam Muslim narrated from Anas that he said:

"By Allah, my wealth is indeed abundant. And indeed, today my children and my grandchildren number nearly one hundred."

And in Sahih Bukhari:

"For I am indeed among the wealthiest of the Ansar."

Abu Al-Aliya said:

"And he (i.e., Anas) had a garden that produced fruit twice a year, and it had basil, from which he would smell the fragrance of musk."

Imam Abu Nu'aim narrated from Hafsa bint Sirin about Anas, who said:

"My land produces fruit twice a year, and no other land in the city produces fruit twice."

May Allah include us, our brothers and sisters, and our descendants among those who seek sustenance with these supplications and receive abundant and pure sustenance. Ameen, O Ever-Living, O Sustainer.

Summary of the Book

1. Seeking Forgiveness and Repentance: This involves not only repeating the words of forgiveness and repentance but also requires distancing oneself from sins, feeling remorse for past wrongdoings, and making a firm and sincere intention not to approach them again until the end of one's life. Such repentance will bring down the rain of mercy, increase wealth and offspring, provide lush gardens and water-filled canals, end drought, eradicate poverty, and replace the dryness of gardens with abundance. It will also enhance strength, grant relief from sorrows, and rescue from difficulties.

2. Piety: Piety is not merely a claim of righteousness but involves protecting oneself from everything that leads to sin, adhering to Allah's commands and prohibitions, and avoiding every statement, action, and belief that would make one deserving of divine punishment. Those who are pious will be granted relief from every sorrow in this world and the Hereafter, sustenance from unexpected sources, and blessings from the heavens and the earth, which will be eternal and free from any evil.

3. Reliance on Allah: Reliance does not mean abandoning efforts to earn sustenance, but rather it means having faith that everything in the universe happens according to Allah's will and command. One's trust should be in the grace and mercy of the Lord of Glory, not merely in the struggle to earn a living. Those who rely on Allah are provided with sustenance like birds, who leave their nests empty in the morning and return with full bellies by evening.

4. Devotion to Worship: This does not mean spending the entire day and night in the mosque and avoiding efforts to earn a living. Instead, it means being present with heart and soul in worship, having humility

and devotion, and being aware of the communion with the Lord of Glory. Allah provides such worshippers with their needs, fills their hearts with affluence, and their hands with sustenance.

5. Following up with Hajj and Umrah: This means performing Umrah after Hajj and Hajj after Umrah. Continually doing so will remove sins, poverty, and neediness as a furnace removes rust from iron, gold, and silver.

6. Maintaining Family Ties: This involves treating relatives with kindness, showing compassion and empathy, and taking care of their needs. Maintaining family ties is not limited to financial help but includes every effort to bring good to relatives and protect them from harm. Greeting relatives with peace is also part of maintaining family ties. The best way to maintain ties with unfaithful and bad relatives is to use all efforts, energy, and resources to save them from the fire of Hell. Maintaining family ties is the quickest way to obtain good rewards in this world. It leads to relief from poverty, love in the family, increased sustenance, blessings in life, increased strength, and protection from a bad death.

7. Spending in the Way of Allah: This refers to spending in accordance with the teachings of religion, such as giving to the poor and supporting the cause of the faith. Spending in the way of Allah is promised by the Lord of the worlds to yield good rewards in this world and the Hereafter. Every morning, an angel prays for the best return for those who spend in the way of Allah. There are many examples in hadith literature and daily life showing the best rewards for those who spend in the way of Allah.

8. Spending on Those Dedicated to Acquiring Religious Knowledge: Spending on scholars increases the value of the spent money as it aids them in acquiring knowledge. Some scholars of the Ummah, after the

prophetic mission, considered the scholars' position as the highest and used to spend their charity on those among them who were deserving.

9. Kindness to the Weak: Honoring and aiding the weak and helpless Muslims results in Allah's support against enemies and opens the doors to sustenance.

10. Migration for the Sake of Allah: This means migrating from the abode of disbelief to the abode of faith, for the purpose of establishing religion and supporting the believers against disbelievers who oppress them. It results in freedom from sorrows, guidance instead of misguidance, and affluence in place of poverty from the Lord, who grants relief to the hearts, broadens guidance, and bestows wealth.

The summary of the discussion regarding the remaining keys to sustenance is as follows:

1. Making the Hereafter the Main Goal: This does not mean abandoning efforts for livelihood but prioritizing the Hereafter as the main goal. One should not compromise the Hereafter for the sake of this world. By making the Hereafter the focus, Allah places affluence in the heart, organizes scattered affairs, and makes the world come to such a person as insignificant. Poverty is removed from his forehead, and he lives in affluence, starting and ending his day with it. His means of sustenance suffices him.

2. Following the Book of Allah: Adhering to it brings breadth and expansion from all directions. It results in rain of mercy from the sky and provision of grains, plants, fruits, and other blessings from the earth.

3. Excellence: This means complying with divine commands in all aspects of life. Those who do so are granted by Allah not only goodness in the Hereafter but also in this world, including ample sustenance, a pleasant life, heart's tranquility, peace, and happiness.

4: Faith and Righteous Deeds: Allah grants every good deed its reward in this world before the Hereafter. He bestows upon the believers who perform righteous deeds the great blessing of a good life, which encompasses pure and lawful sustenance, happiness, contentment, worship, the ability to obey the Lord of Glory, and the expansion of the heart for it.

5: Commanding Family Members to Pray and Observing It Diligently: Those who instruct their family members to establish prayer and themselves diligently adhere to it will find their efforts in earning sustenance blessed and fruitful. Allah provides them with means of sustenance from sources they could not even imagine.

6: Remembrance of (Subhan Allah wa bihamdiHi): This is considered the prayer of everything, and creation is provided sustenance based on it. Prophet Noah (peace be upon him) instructed his son to recite this at the time of his death, and the Prophet Muhammad (peace be upon him) informed the Ummah of this advice so that they too may seek sustenance through it.

7: Marriage: Unmarried individuals, despite their financial struggles, should marry with the intention of obeying the Lord and avoiding the forbidden. There is clear and explicit glad tidings in the Quran and Sunnah for such individuals to attain wealth and affluence. This glad tidings does not imply that those who marry should abandon their efforts for sustenance or cease their current endeavors. Rather, it means that Allah will enable such individuals to find ways and means to earn a livelihood so that supporting the family formed through marriage will not become a problem.

8: Leaving Early in the Morning: The Prophet Muhammad (peace be upon him) prayed for blessings for those who seek sustenance early in the morning. He himself used to send his military troops and armies early in the morning. Allah blessed the narrator of this Hadith with wealth by starting their business endeavors early in the morning. Overcoming the major obstacle of insufficient sleep (by adopting the habit of sleeping early) should be pursued to facilitate early morning efforts.

9: Truthfulness in Transactions and Disclosure of Defects: Ensuring truthfulness and disclosing defects in buying and selling brings blessings. The pious find comfort and expansion in this world due to their adherence to these practices before receiving their reward in the Hereafter.

10: Measuring Grain: Following the Sunnah of the Prophet Muhammad (peace be upon him) by measuring grain during transactions brings blessings. Although there are differing opinions among hadith scholars regarding the necessity of measuring grain, the prevailing view is that measuring grain in such cases is a means of obtaining blessings.

11: Genuine Intention to Repay Debt: Allah assists and supports those who sincerely intend to repay their debts, providing them with a protector and means of sustenance. There are examples of the benefits of such intentions in the hadith literature and daily life.

12-17:

- Entering the Home with a Greeting: Entering the home while greeting.

- Going to the Mosque: Going to the mosque.

- Being in the Congregational Prayer Mosque: Being in a mosque where congregational prayers are held.

- Going Out for Jihad: Going out for the sake of Allah.

- Visiting the Sick: Visiting the sick.

- Accompanying a Funeral: Accompanying a funeral.

- Supporting the Ruler in Justice: Supporting the ruler in matters of justice.

- Staying Home Without Backbiting: Staying home without engaging in backbiting.

For those who engage in these eight acts, their Lord is the guarantor. If they remain alive, Allah provides them with sustenance, suffices their sorrows and worries, and if they pass away, He promises to admit them into paradise.

18: Establishing Legal Limits: Establishing legal limits involves eliminating evil and opening the doors of divine mercy. The end of evil and the opening of divine mercy bring about expansion in sustenance and comfort in livelihood.

19: Steadfastness: Steadfastness in obedience to Allah in every situation, at all times, and in every place leads to abundance, expansion, and an increase in sustenance in this world before the Hereafter.

20: Proven Supplications for Seeking Sustenance: The previous prophets and the final Prophet Muhammad (peace be upon him) used to make supplications to Allah for sustenance. By making supplications that are present in the Quran and Sunnah, there is strong hope of being granted acceptance in the divine presence.

And since the obligations that God Almighty has imposed on His servants are the most beloved acts to Him, performing them is the most beloved thing to Him and the strongest means of drawing close to Him, as mentioned in the hadith of Abu Huraira - may God be pleased with him - in Al-Bukhari and the hadith of Aisha - may God be pleased with her - in Ahmad, that the Prophet, peace and blessings be upon him, said: "My servant draws not near to Me with anything more loved by Me than the religious duties I have imposed upon him, and My servant continues to draw near to Me with supererogatory works so that I shall love him. When I love him, I am his hearing with which he hears, his sight with which he sees, his hand with which he strikes, and his foot with which he walks. Were he to ask [something] of Me, I would surely give it to him, and were he to ask Me for refuge, I would surely grant him it." This wording is from Al-Bukhari, and Ahmad's wording is similar.

Among the most prominent obligations and acts of worship that bring the servant closer to his Master after faith and piety, and that bring about the blessings of this world and the Hereafter, and blessings in provision and happiness in life and after death, are, for example: (prayer, pilgrimage and 'Umrah, zakat, charity, and maintaining kinship ties).

1 - Prayer:

God Almighty said: {O you who have believed, seek help through patience and prayer. Indeed, Allah is with the patient} 4. And He said: {Recite, [O Muhammad], what has been revealed to you of the Book and establish prayer. Indeed, prayer prohibits immorality and wrongdoing}.

And He said: {And I did not create the jinn and mankind except to worship Me. I do not want from them any provision, nor do I want them to feed Me. Indeed, it is Allah who is the [continual] Provider, the firm possessor of strength}. And He also said: {And enjoin prayer upon your family [and people] and be steadfast therein. We ask you not for provision; We provide for you, and the [best] outcome is for [those of] righteousness}.

Al-Hafiz Ibn Kathir said: "His saying: {We ask you not for provision; We provide for you} means if you establish prayer, provision will come to you from where you do not expect, as He said: {And whoever fears Allah - He will make for him a way out. And will provide for him from where he does not expect}, and He said: {And I did not create the jinn and mankind except to worship Me}."

It came in Al-Tirmidhi, Ibn Majah, and Ahmad in the hadith: "Indeed, Allah, the Exalted, says: O son of Adam, devote yourself to My worship, I will fill your heart with contentment and take care of your poverty. If you do not do so, I will fill your hands with problems and will not take care of your poverty." Al-Tirmidhi considered it good, and the wording is his, and similar wording is in Ahmad and Ibn Majah, where "your heart" replaces "your hands". Al-Albani said: It is authentic

.

And in Al-Tirmidhi also, from the hadith of Anas - may God be pleased with him: "Whoever has the Hereafter as his concern, God will place richness in his heart, gather his affairs, and the world will come to him unwillingly. And whoever has the world as his concern, God will place poverty before his eyes, disband his affairs, and he will get nothing of the world except what was decreed for him." Al-Albani said it is authentic.

Ibn Qayyim al-Jawziyyah said: "Prayer is one of the greatest aids in obtaining the benefits of this world and the Hereafter, and in repelling the harms of this world and the Hereafter. It forbids immorality, removes the ailments of the hearts, expels disease from the body, illuminates the heart, whitens the face, activates the limbs and the soul, brings provision, repels oppression, supports the oppressed, subdues the mixture of desires, preserves blessings, repels misfortunes, brings down mercy, and removes distress".

Al-Munawi said: "Prayer helps in repelling all calamities by the assistance of the Creator who intended it as a means to turn to Him and draw near to Him. So whoever turns to Him completely with prayer, He will protect and suffice him for turning away from everything else, and that is the nature of every great person regarding anyone who turns to him with his whole being".

2 - Pilgrimage and 'Umrah:

It has been established from him, peace be upon him, that alternating between pilgrimage and 'Umrah causes wealth and repels poverty. It was mentioned in the hadith of Ibn Mas'ud - may God be pleased with him - and others in both Al-Tirmidhi, Al-Nasa'i, and Ibn Majah (the latter from the hadith of Umar - may God be pleased with him), and Ahmad, that he, peace be upon him, said: "Alternate between pilgrimage and 'Umrah, for they eliminate poverty and sins as the bellows eliminate impurity from iron, gold, and silver. And there is no reward for an accepted pilgrimage except Paradise."

Al-Mubarakfuri said: "His saying: 'They eliminate poverty' may mean apparent poverty by obtaining wealth and hidden poverty by obtaining contentment of the heart".

3 - Zakat and related charities and maintaining kinship ties:

As for zakat, God - Almighty - has made it a purification for wealth and its owner and a guarantee of the blessing for the wealthy. The blessing of wealth remains for those who pay their zakat, and God preserves it for them, increases it, and repels calamities and disasters from them with it, making it a wall and a strong fortress and a faithful guard for them.

Therefore, He said: {Take from their wealth a charity by which you purify them and cause them increase, and invoke blessings upon them. Indeed, your invocations are reassurance for them. And Allah is Hearing and Knowing}.

When this verse was revealed: {And those who hoard gold and silver}, he said: "This was difficult for the Muslims." And in it, the Prophet, peace be upon him, said: "God only imposed zakat to purify what remains of your wealth, and He imposed inheritance to be for those who come after you."

And He, the Almighty, said: {And whatever you give for charity, desiring the face of Allah - it is they who will get a manifold increase}.

Al-Qurtubi said: "In its meaning are two sayings: one is that their good deeds are multiplied for them, and the other is that they have been given much good and blessings, meaning they are the ones with manifold blessings".

As for voluntary charities, spending, and maintaining kinship ties - which sometimes include obligatory charity - Islam has given great importance to these. The Master of mankind, peace be upon him, was the greatest in charity with what he owned. He would give as someone who did not fear poverty, and his joy in giving was greater than the joy of the recipient. He would prefer others over himself, all this while diversifying his methods of giving according to the situations and circumstances of those he was giving to. He taught his companions this and commanded them, and he would pray for the charitable among them, bringing blessings to what they spent and to them from the blessings of his prayers, peace be upon him.

There are many verses and hadiths that show that charity, spending, and maintaining kinship ties are reasons for bringing provision, obtaining blessings, and the continuity of blessings. Among them is His saying: {Allah destroys interest and gives increase for charities}. His saying: {gives increase for charities} means He blesses them in this world and increases their reward by multiplying it in the Hereafter.

And He, the Almighty, said: {Satan threatens you with poverty and orders you to immorality, while Allah promises you forgiveness from Him and bounty. And Allah is all-Encompassing and Knowing}.

Meaning that Satan threatens and makes a person fear poverty and loss of wealth by paying zakat, and orders him to commit sins and abandon acts of obedience.

While Allah - Almighty - promises the believers forgiveness of their sins and covering them by giving charity, He also promises to replace what they give and to bestow upon them from His bounties and to shower them with provisions.

And Ibn Atiyyah said in the meaning of His saying: {And Allah promises you forgiveness from Him and bounty}, forgiveness is the covering over His servants in this world and the Hereafter, and the bounty is provision in this world and its expansion and the bliss in the Hereafter.

And He, the Almighty, said: {And whatever you spend of anything, He will replace it, and He is the best of providers}. Al-Qurtubi said: "This is an indication that the replacement in this world is similar to what is spent if the expenditure is in obedience to Allah, and Allah, the Almighty, provides from inexhaustible and endless treasures."

And Ibn Kathir said: "He will replace it for you with a substitute, and in the Hereafter with reward and recompense." Among the hadiths with this meaning is what came in Muslim from the hadith of Abu Hurairah - may Allah be pleased with him - that the Prophet, peace be upon him, said: "Allah, the Blessed and Exalted, said: O son of Adam, spend, and I will spend on you." And in another hadith, the Messenger of Allah, peace be upon him, said: "Indeed, Allah said to me: Spend, and I will spend on you."

Al-Bukhari, Muslim, and Ahmad narrated the hadith of Abu Hurairah - may Allah be pleased with him - that the Prophet, peace be upon him, said: "No day passes in which the servants wake up but two angels descend. One of them says: O Allah, give the spender a replacement, and the other says: O Allah, give the withholder destruction." This is the wording of Al-Bukhari and Muslim, and it is in Ahmad with a similar wording.

Ibn Hajar mentioned that the hadith encourages spending in ways of goodness and that it is promised to be replaced in the immediate with increase and in the Hereafter with reward.

Al-Nawawi said: "The commendable spending here is that which is in obedience and on dependents, guests, and voluntary acts."

Al-Qurtubi said: "It includes obligations and recommendations."

And from Abu Hurairah - may Allah be pleased with him - and others with an elevated (marfu') chain, in it the wording: "Spend, Bilal, and do not fear from the One who has the Throne any decrease," narrated by Al-Bazzar, Al-Tabarani, Abu Nu'aym, and Al-Bayhaqi in Shu'ab, and in some of them from the hadith of Bilal and Ibn Mas'ud with similar wording as well.

And the hadith of Asma bint Abi Bakr, may Allah be pleased with them both, narrated by Al-Bukhari, Muslim, Abu Dawood, Al-Tirmidhi, Al-Nasa'i, Ahmad, Abd Al-Razzaq, and Al-Bayhaqi that the Messenger of Allah, peace be upon him, said to her: "Spend and do not count, so Allah will count for you, and do not hoard, so Allah will hoard for you." This is the wording of Al-Bukhari, Muslim, and Ahmad, except that it is said in Muslim: "Give freely or spend or expend and do not count...", and in these - also - and in others with similar wording. Some have only mentioned the first part or the second part of the hadith.

Al-Nawawi said: "And do not count..." meaning: He will prevent you as you prevented, He will withhold from you as you withheld, and He will hold back His favor from you as you held it back. It is also said that 'do not count' means do not consider it too much so that it causes you to stop spending.

Ibn Hajar said: "The prohibition is against withholding charity out of fear of depletion, for that is one of the greatest causes of cutting off the source of blessing. For Allah rewards giving without reckoning, and whoever does not reckon in reward is not reckoned against in giving. One who knows that Allah provides from unexpected sources should give without reckoning. Counting means to keep something to store and not spend from it, and Allah will cut off the blessing or withhold provision or reckon with it in the Hereafter."

Al-Sindi said: Do not withhold what is in your hand so that Allah may tighten the doors of provision on you. This indicates that generosity opens the doors of provision, while miserliness does the opposite.

Al-Mubarakfuri said: "The hadith indicates that charity increases wealth and becomes a cause of blessing and increase in it. Whoever is miserly and does not give charity, Allah will withhold blessing and increase from their wealth."

The hadith of Abu Hurairah - may Allah be pleased with him - narrated by Muslim, Al-Tirmidhi, Al-Darimi, and Ahmad with the wording: "Charity does not decrease wealth, and Allah increases His servant in honor when they forgive, and no one humbles themselves for Allah except that Allah raises them." Al-Tirmidhi said: The hadith is good and authentic.

I say: This is the wording of Muslim, Al-Tirmidhi, and Al-Darimi, and the wording of Ahmad is similar.

The meaning of "Charity does not decrease wealth" is that charity does not decrease wealth, or part of it, or anything from it, but rather it increases many times over by being compensated with hidden blessings, by warding off harms, by apparent gifts, or by elevated rewards.

The hadith of Abu Hurairah - may Allah be pleased with him - narrated by Al-Bukhari, Muslim, and others: "The example of a miser and a spender is like two men wearing iron cloaks from their chests to their collarbones. As for the spender, he does not spend except that it spreads and covers his skin so much that it hides his fingertips and erases his traces. As for the miser, he does not want to spend anything except that each ring of the cloak sticks to its place, and he tries to expand it but it does not expand." This is the wording of Al-Bukhari, and it is narrated by Muslim with similar wording.

The hadith shows that the spender is covered by Allah with his spending, hiding his flaws in this world and the Hereafter, and his wealth is increased by charity and spending, just as this cloak covers and fits its wearer. As for the miser, it is as if he wore a cloak that only covers his chest, leaving him exposed and disgraced in this world and the Hereafter by the depletion of his wealth in this world and the loss of his good deeds in the Hereafter.

What is worth noting here is that praying for the one who gives charity and spends money has great importance in bringing growth and blessings. The Prophet, peace be upon him, used to pray for those who paid zakat or charity and would instruct his workers to pray for those who spent money as well. We have a good example in the Messenger of Allah, peace be upon him.

Abdullah bin Abi Awfa, may Allah be pleased with him, said: "When the Messenger of Allah, peace be upon him, received people with their charity, he said: 'O Allah, send prayers upon them.' My father came to him with his charity and he said: 'O Allah, send prayers upon the family of Abu Awfa'". He meant here to pray for him. He would sometimes say: "O Allah, bless him and his camels" if the charity was camels, and so on.

As for keeping the ties of kinship: Allah Almighty has commanded keeping the ties of kinship, which is to be kind to relatives in words and deeds and to spend money on them. The noble Messenger, peace be upon him, emphasized this and explained that keeping the ties of kinship has many benefits, such as an increase in lifespan, provision, good reputation, and high ranks in the Hereafter by Allah's grace and generosity. The evidence for this is His saying: {Would you then, if you were given authority, do mischief in the land, and sever your ties of kinship? Those are the ones whom Allah has cursed, so He made them deaf and blinded their sight}.

Abu Huraira, may Allah be pleased with him, narrated from Al-Bukhari and Muslim and others in several ways and words: "Allah created the creation, and when He finished it, the womb stood up and took hold of the Rahman. He said to it: 'What is it?' It said: 'This is the place of one seeking refuge from severance.' He said: 'Will you not be pleased that I keep ties with the one who keeps ties with you and sever ties with the one who severs ties with you?' It said: 'Yes, O Lord.' He said: 'That is for you.'" Abu Huraira said: "Recite if you wish: {Would you then, if you were given authority, do mischief in the land, and sever your ties of kinship? Those are the ones whom Allah has cursed, so He made them deaf and blinded their sight}" This is the wording of Al-Bukhari, and with Muslim in a similar, shortened version.

And the hadith of Abu Huraira, may Allah be pleased with him, in Al-Bukhari, and the hadith of Aisha, may Allah be pleased with her, in Muslim, both narrated and raised: "The womb is a branch from the Rahman. Allah said: 'Whoever keeps ties with you, I will keep ties with him, and whoever severs ties with you, I will sever ties with him.'" This is the wording of Al-Bukhari, and with Muslim in a similar manner.

And the hadith of Abdul-Rahman bin Awf, may Allah be pleased with him, in Al-Tirmidhi, narrated and raised: Allah the Blessed and Exalted said: "I am Allah, and I am the Rahman. I created the womb and derived its name from My name. Whoever keeps ties with it, I will keep ties with him, and whoever severs ties with it, I will sever ties with him." Al-Tirmidhi said: The hadith is authentic.

And the hadith of Abdullah bin Amr in both Al-Bukhari and Al-Tirmidhi, narrated and raised with the wording: "The one who maintains kinship is not the one who recompenses, but the one who maintains kinship is the one who, when his kinship is severed, he keeps it." This is the wording of Al-Bukhari, and Al-Tirmidhi similarly except that he said: "when his kinship is cut off" instead of "when his kinship is severed." Al-Tirmidhi commented: The hadith is good and authentic, and in the chapter, there are also narrations from Salman and Aisha.

Among the narrations that indicate maintaining family ties as a cause for bringing provision and blessings is the hadith of Anas bin Malik, may Allah be pleased with him, from the Prophet, peace be upon him, who said: "Whoever would like his provision to be expanded and his lifespan to be extended, let him maintain his family ties." And in another wording: "Whoever loves that his provision be expanded and his lifespan be extended, let him maintain his family ties." This is found in Al-Bukhari, Muslim, and similarly in Abu Dawud.

In the hadith of Abu Huraira, may Allah be pleased with him, narrated and raised by both Al-Tirmidhi, Ahmad, Al-Hakim, and others, it includes: "Learn enough of your lineage to maintain your family ties, for maintaining family ties brings love among relatives, increases wealth, and extends lifespan."

From the above - and through careful consideration of the scholars' explanations of the hadiths - we can conclude the following:

1. The emphasis on maintaining family ties and that Allah Almighty derived its name from His name, the Most Glorious.

And that He placed it under His protection and safeguard, and Allah's neighbor is not forsaken.

2 - The prohibition of severing family ties, and that the one who severs them is cut off from the mercy of Allah, the Exalted, and His great kindness, forsaken in this world and the hereafter.

3 - The family ties that Allah commanded to be maintained are both general and specific. The general family ties pertain to the religion and must be maintained with affection, advice, justice, fairness, and fulfilling obligatory and recommended rights.

As for the specific family ties, they go beyond the general ones, involving spending on relatives, looking after their conditions, overlooking their faults, fulfilling their needs, protecting them from harm, showing cheerfulness, and praying for them if they are righteous and upright. If they are sinners and immoral, then boycotting them after exhausting efforts to advise them is their connection, while praying for their guidance in their absence.

4 - As for the benefit of maintaining family ties, which is the crux of the matter here, it is that the one who maintains them will always be connected with great kindness from the Most Merciful, by receiving provision, warding off harm, continual blessings, success in life, and joy and happiness after death. This is often observed and experienced, and people talk about it and recognize it. The previous hadiths of Abu Huraira and Anas, may Allah be pleased with them, indicated that the one who maintains ties will have their provision expanded.

Al-Nawawi said: "Expanding provision means broadening and increasing it, and it is said that it is blessing in it". And Al-Hafiz Ibn Hajar said: The scholars said: The meaning of expanding provision is blessing in it because maintaining ties with relatives is a charity, and charity increases wealth and makes it grow.

The second topic:

Reliance on Allah - exalted is He - while taking the means

The essence of reliance is the heart's dependence on Allah to obtain what benefits the servant in his religion and worldly life and to ward off what harms him in his religion and worldly life. This reliance and certainty must be accompanied by taking the means that Allah has set as causes for their effects, both by divine decree and law. Neglecting these means undermines the very nature of reliance and nullifies wisdom and law.

Reliance comes after attaining piety as a result of it and a necessary consequence. Therefore, Allah says: {And fear Allah, and upon Allah let the believers rely.}, and He also says: {And whoever fears Allah - He will make for him a way out, and will provide for him from where he does not expect. And whoever relies upon Allah - then He is sufficient for him.}.

Thus, Allah has made reliance follow piety, which involves carrying out the commanded means. Then, if one relies on Allah, He will be sufficient for him and will suffice him.

Al-Qurtubi said: "Reliance is trust in Allah and the certainty that His decree is in force, while following the way of His Prophet in striving for the necessary means such as food and drink, protecting oneself from an enemy, and preparing...". And Imam Al-Qushayri said: "Know that reliance is in the heart, while outward action does not contradict reliance in the heart, as long as the servant realizes that provision comes from Allah. If something is difficult, it is by His decree, and if something is easy, it is by His facilitation."

Allah mentioned the stance of the Prophet and his companions when some people tried to frighten them with their enemies, the Quraysh and their allies, by saying: {Those to whom people said, "Indeed, the people have gathered against you, so fear them." But it [merely] increased them in faith, and they said, "Sufficient for us is Allah, and [He is] the best Disposer of affairs." So they returned with favor from

Allah and bounty, no harm having touched them. And they pursued the pleasure of Allah, and Allah is the possessor of great bounty.}. Thus, some people tried to frighten them with their enemies, the polytheists of Makkah and their allies, but the believers said: {Sufficient for us is Allah, and [He is] the best Disposer of affairs.} They relied on Allah after taking the means, so Allah sufficed them and warded off the harm intended by their enemies after the battle of Uhud, and they returned with the blessing of safety and increased bounty from Allah, profiting from the market.

The Prophet, peace be upon him, was the leader of those who relied on his Lord, commanding reliance on Allah and turning to Him after taking the means in all circumstances. An example of this from his tradition is found in the hadith of Imran bin Husayn, may Allah be pleased with him, who said: The Messenger of Allah, peace be upon him, said: "Whoever devotes himself to Allah, Allah will suffice him for all his needs and provide for him from where he does not expect, and whoever devotes himself to the world, Allah will entrust him to it."

And the hadith of Abdullah bin Mas'ud, may Allah be pleased with him, raised by Abu Dawood, Al-Tirmidhi, Ahmad, Al-Tabarani, and Al-Hakim with the wording: "Whoever is afflicted with poverty and brings it to people, his poverty will not be alleviated. And whoever is afflicted with poverty and brings it to Allah, Allah will soon provide him with immediate or delayed provision." In another wording: "Whoever is afflicted with a need and brings it to people, his need will not be easily met. And whoever brings it to Allah, Allah will provide for him with immediate or delayed provision." The first wording is from Al-Tirmidhi, and the other from Ahmad, and the others have similar versions. Al-Tirmidhi said after it: "A good, authentic, and unique hadith." Al-Hakim said after it: "An authentic chain of narration, but they did not narrate it," and Al-Dhahabi agreed with him.

In this hadith, it is shown that whoever is in severe need due to poverty or difficulty and presents it to people and complains about it to them, seeking to have his need alleviated by them, his poverty will not be alleviated, and his need will not be fulfilled. Thus, whenever one need is fulfilled, another greater need befalls him. But if he presents it to Allah and relies on his Master, Allah will hasten to provide for him and quickly grant him immediate provision, which is wealth and sufficiency, or a close death of a wealthy relative so he inherits from him.

Ibn Abbas, may Allah be pleased with them, said: "I was behind the Prophet, peace be upon him, one day, and he said: 'O boy, I will teach you some words: Preserve Allah, He will preserve you. Preserve Allah, you will find Him before you. If you ask, ask Allah. If you seek help, seek help from Allah. Know that if the nation were to gather together to benefit you with something, they would not benefit you except with something that Allah has written for you. And if they gathered together to harm you with something, they would not harm you except with something that Allah has written against you. The pens have been lifted, and the pages have dried.' Narrated by Al-Tirmidhi and Ahmad, and this wording is from Al-Tirmidhi, and the wording from Ahmad is similar. Al-Tirmidhi said after it: 'A good and authentic hadith.'"

Al-Tirmidhi also mentioned in the same chapter the hadith of Anas, may Allah be pleased with him: A man said to the Prophet, peace be upon him: "O Messenger of Allah, should I tie it and rely upon Allah, or let it go and rely upon Allah?" He said: "Tie it and rely upon Allah," meaning his camel.

Habbah and Sawa' bin Khalid, may Allah be pleased with them, said: "We entered upon the Prophet, peace be upon him, while he was handling something, so we helped him with it. He said: 'Do not despair of provision as long as your heads are moving, for a person is born by his mother with nothing on him, then Allah provides for him.'" Narrated by Ibn Majah, Ibn Hibban, Ahmad, and Al-Tabarani, and the wording is with them except for Ibn Hibban, who narrated it with a similar wording. Al-Busiri said: "The chain of their hadith is authentic; its men are trustworthy." But Ibn Hajar said: "The hadith was narrated by Ibn Majah with a good chain."

Al-Tirmidhi, Ibn Majah, Ahmad, and Al-Hakim narrated the hadith of Umar bin Al-Khattab, may Allah be pleased with him, who said: "I heard the Messenger of Allah say: 'If you were to rely upon Allah with the reliance He is due, He would provide for you as He provides for the birds; they go out in the morning hungry and return in the evening full.'" This wording is from Ibn Majah and Ahmad in the second place, as well as Al-Hakim. With Al-Tirmidhi and Ahmad in the first place: "If you were to rely upon Allah with true reliance."

Thus, it becomes clear from the above that reliance and devotion to Allah is a reason for obtaining provision, blessing in it, fulfilling needs, and alleviating hardship and distress by Allah's permission.

And he said: In the name of Allah, O Allah, keep the devil away from us and keep the devil away from what You have provided us, so they were blessed with a child, and the devil did not harm him."

The most explicit hadith regarding the command to say the name of Allah, especially when eating, is what came from Abu Dawood, Al-Tirmidhi, Al-Hakim, and others from the hadith of Aisha, may Allah be pleased with her, that the Prophet, peace be upon him, said: "When one of you eats, let him mention the name of Allah. If he forgets to mention the name of Allah at the beginning, let him say: In the name of Allah at its beginning and end." This is the wording of Abu Dawood, and in Al-Tirmidhi and Al-Hakim it is similar. Al-Hakim said afterward: It has an authentic chain of narration and they did not narrate it, and Al-Dhahabi agreed with him, and Ibn Qayyim Al-Jawziyya also authenticated it.

It has also been narrated by Al-Bukhari, Muslim, and others from the hadith of Umar bin Abi Salama, in which the Prophet, peace be upon him, said to him: "O boy, mention the name of Allah, eat with your right hand, and eat from what is in front of you..."

The benefit of mentioning the name of Allah becomes clear through the following hadiths:

From Abu Huraira, who said: The Messenger of Allah, peace be upon him, said: "Every important matter that does not begin with the name of Allah, the Most Merciful, the Most Compassionate, is cut off." In another wording: "Every important matter that does not begin with the praise of Allah is cut off," and in another narration: "It is amputated." This was narrated by Ibn Majah, Abu Dawood, Ibn Hibban, Al-Daraqutni, and Al-Nasa'i. The second wording is the most frequent and well-known. Its chains of narration were mentioned by Al-Subki, who authenticated it, and Al-Nawawi said: "This hadith is good... It was narrated both connected and disconnected, and the chain of the connected narration is good. The meaning of 'cut off' is that it is devoid of blessing, and likewise 'amputated.'"

The commentator on Sunan Ibn Majah said: Al-Sindi said: "The hadith was authenticated by Ibn Al-Salah and Al-Nawawi."

Al-Hafiz Ibn Hajar, when discussing the letter of the Prophet, peace be upon him, to Heraclius, said: "In it was 'In the name of Allah, the Most Merciful, the Most Compassionate': Al-Nawawi said: 'It is recommended to begin letters with 'In the name of Allah, the Most Merciful, the Most Compassionate,' and his saying in the hadith of Abu Huraira: 'Every important matter that does not begin with the praise of Allah is cut off,' meaning with the mention of Allah, as came in another narration, for it was narrated in different ways: with the mention of Allah, with 'In the name of Allah,' and with 'the praise of Allah.' He said: And this letter was of great importance and was not begun with the word 'praise' but with 'In the name of Allah.'"

And from Jabir bin Abdullah, may Allah be pleased with them, from Muslim, Abu Dawood, Ibn Majah, and Ahmad, that the Prophet, peace be upon him, said: "When a man enters his house and mentions Allah at his entry and when eating, the devil says: 'There is no lodging for you and no dinner.' But if he enters and does not mention Allah at his entry, the devil says: 'You have found lodging,' and if he does not mention Allah when eating, he says: 'You have found lodging and dinner.'" This is the wording of Muslim, and the others have it similarly with some additions at the beginning.

And from Aisha, may Allah be pleased with her, from Al-Tirmidhi and Ibn Majah, she said: "The Messenger of Allah, peace be upon him, was eating food with six of his companions when a Bedouin came and ate it in two bites. The Messenger of Allah, peace be upon him, said: 'If he had mentioned the name of Allah, it would have sufficed for you all.'" This is the wording of Al-Tirmidhi, and the wording of Ibn Majah is similar with some additions. Al-Tirmidhi said afterward: "This hadith is good and authentic," and Al-Albani also authenticated it.

It has been authenticated by Al-Bukhari and narrated by more than one of the companions, may Allah be pleased with them, in an elevated manner: "The believer eats in one intestine, while the disbeliever eats in seven intestines."

From the above, and through looking into the books of hadith explanations, it becomes clear:

1 - The importance of mentioning the name of Allah in every important matter, as it brings goodness and blessings and repels the

accursed devil who eradicates blessings and leads to sin. The importance of mentioning the name of Allah is also indicated by the fact that many who extracted the previous hadiths titled their chapters with the mention of the name of Allah as observed.

2 - It is recommended to mention the name of Allah at the beginning of every significant matter such as entering, exiting, eating, drinking, weighing, measuring, counting money, dressing, and intimate relations, and to praise Allah at the end of it. Al-Nawawi reported the consensus on the recommendation of mentioning the name of Allah and said: The devil is able to eat the food if a person starts it without mentioning the name of Allah. The devil's eating is taken literally because reason does not deem it impossible, and the law has not denied it, but rather affirmed it, so it must be accepted and believed.

3 - It has been said that the meaning of this is that the devil delights in the removal of blessing from that food if the name of Allah is not mentioned over it.

4 - The devil is not given power, by Allah's permission, over those who mention His name due to the blessing of the mention. This is because in the mention of Allah and His supplication, there is a refuge from the devil and his helpers, so the devil does not associate with them or approach them, and thus blessings are obtained.

And constant remembrance and supplication bring all goodness and blessings, repel every affliction and harm, bring one closer to the Most Merciful, attain His pleasure, distance from the devil, and expel him and his helpers. The Messenger of Allah, peace and blessings be upon him, also guided to constant remembrance and supplication, as he would remember Allah at all times and supplicate to his Lord in all conditions for all good of this world and the Hereafter. He would also supplicate for his companions with what benefits them in their religion, worldly life, and Hereafter.

It is narrated by Abu Huraira, may Allah be pleased with him, in Muslim that he, peace and blessings be upon him, used to say, "O Allah, rectify for me my religion which is the safeguard of my affairs, and rectify for me my world wherein is my livelihood..." He, peace and blessings be upon him, also used to say, "O Allah, forgive my sin, widen my abode, and bless me in what You have provided me," reported by Tirmidhi, Ahmad, Nasa'i, and Ibn al-Sunni, with the wording of Tirmidhi and the rest in a similar manner.

A Bedouin came to the Messenger of Allah, peace and blessings be upon him, as in the hadith of Sa'd ibn Abi Waqqas in Muslim, and said: Teach me some words I can say. He said, "Say: There is no deity but Allah, alone, with no partner, Allah is the Greatest, greatly, and praise be to Allah abundantly, Glory be to Allah, the Lord of the worlds, there is no power nor strength except in Allah, the Mighty, the Wise." He said: These are for my Lord, what is for me? He said, "Say: O Allah, forgive me, have mercy on me, guide me, and provide for me."

And it is reported by Ahmad, Tirmidhi, and Hakim from the hadith of Abu Wa'il, who said that a man came to Ali, may Allah be pleased with him, and said: O Commander of the Believers, I am unable to fulfill my contract of manumission, so help me. Ali, may Allah be pleased with him, said: Shall I not teach you words the Messenger of Allah, peace and blessings be upon him, taught me? If you had a debt as large as Mount Thabir in gold, Allah would pay it off for you. He said: Yes. He said, "Say: O Allah, suffice me with Your lawful against Your unlawful, and enrich me by Your bounty from others besides You." This is the wording of Ahmad, and the wording of Tirmidhi is similar, and Tirmidhi graded it as good, as did Albani. Hakim said: Its chain of narration is authentic and it was not included by the two [Bukhari and Muslim], and Dhahabi agreed with him.

It is authenticated in Sahih Bukhari from the hadith of Anas, may Allah be pleased with him, that the Prophet, peace and blessings be upon him, supplicated for him, saying, "O Allah, increase his wealth and offspring, and bless him in what You have given him."

It is reported by Imam Ahmad from the hadith of Abdullah ibn Amr, may Allah be pleased with them both, and it mentions the advice of Noah, peace be upon him, to his two sons when death approached him, and part of what he said was: "I command you with 'There is no deity but Allah'... and I command you with 'Glory be to Allah and His praise,' for it is the prayer of everything, and by it everything is provided for." Iraqi said: Its chain of narration is authentic, and Haythami said: The men of Ahmad are trustworthy.

Thus, it is clearly shown the great importance of remembrance and supplication in bringing goodness and blessings, repelling disliked and needy conditions, and distancing the devil and humiliating him and his soldiers. Therefore, a person should adhere to constant remembrance and supplication to attain happiness in both the Hereafter and worldly life alike, and Allah knows best.

[Thanking and Praising Allah]

Thankfulness: It is using the blessings of Allah in what pleases Him, as Al-Ghazali said. He also stated in another place, "The existence of an increase in wealth is a blessing, and its thankfulness is to spend it on good deeds or not to use it in disobedience." Ibn Al-Qayyim said, "Thankfulness is the manifestation of Allah's blessing on His servant's tongue, in the form of praise and acknowledgment, in his heart, by witnessing and loving, and on his limbs, by obedience and compliance." Al-Qurtubi said something similar.

Some scholars have partially differentiated between praise and thankfulness, considering them generally and specifically distinct from each other. However, Abu Ja'far Al-Tabari preferred the view that praise may be expressed in the context of thankfulness, and thankfulness may be placed in the context of praise. If this were not the case, it would not be permissible to say, "Praise be to Allah in thanks."

Therefore, Al-Tabari interpreted {Al-Hamdulillah} in Surah Al-Fatiha as pure thankfulness to Allah for the blessings He has bestowed upon His servants, which cannot be counted, and no one else can enumerate them.

These numerous blessings, which cannot be counted or fully comprehended, including the blessing of wealth, necessitate thankfulness from the creation to the Creator, the Provider, the Benefactor. This thankfulness and praise to Him, the Exalted, is a reason for the increase and blessing in wealth, by His grace and favor.

Ibn Al-Qayyim said, "Allah made thankfulness a cause for more of His grace, a guard and preserver of His blessing, and a connector of the thankful to the One thanked."

It should be noted here that some people narrow the meaning of thankfulness, thinking its extent is merely saying with the tongue "Praise be to Allah" or "Thanks be to Allah" and the like, while not using the blessing in disobedience, even if they do not direct the blessing towards obedience. This undoubtedly shows a deficiency in understanding and following the righteous predecessors.

In reality, thankfulness encompasses a wider scope and a broader field. For example, prayer is thankfulness, fasting is thankfulness, and every good deed a person does for Allah is thankfulness. The servant's feeling of modesty due to the continuous blessings is thankfulness, his acknowledgment of shortcomings in thanking the Benefactor, and his apology for his shortcomings is also thankfulness. Talking about Allah's blessing is thankfulness, recognizing that the blessing is a gift from Allah even though he does not deserve it is thankfulness, humility towards the blessings and submission in them to the Benefactor is thankfulness, and minimizing objections, good manners with the Benefactor, receiving the blessing with good acceptance, even if it is simple or little, and considering it great without belittling or minimizing it is thankfulness. The certainty that thankfulness itself is a blessing from Allah and His success is thankfulness, and the best thankfulness is praising Allah.

Allah, the Exalted, commanded His servants to be thankful, and He coupled thankfulness with remembrance. He said, {So remember Me; I will remember you. And be grateful to Me and do not deny Me.} He also promised a reward for thankfulness, even assuring more with thankfulness. He said, {And We will surely reward the grateful.} And He said, {If you are grateful, I will surely increase you [in favor]; but if you deny, indeed, My punishment is severe.} And He said, {But as for the favor of your Lord, report [it].} And He also said, {And few of My servants are grateful.}

The statements of the scholars and interpreters regarding these verses support and confirm the previous meanings of thanking Allah, the Exalted. Abu Ja'far Al-Tabari said about His saying, {And be grateful to Me and do not deny Me}, meaning, do not deny My favor upon you, so I take away My blessing that I have given you. Rather, be thankful to Me for it, and I will increase you, complete My blessing upon you, and guide you to what I have guided to those of My servants whom I have accepted. For I promised My creation that whoever is thankful to Me, I will increase him, and whoever denies Me, I will deprive him and take away what I have given him.

Abu Ja'far's statement here, "And whoever denies Me," does not necessarily mean the disbeliever in the literal sense, as opposed to the Muslim. Rather, it refers to a broader category, including those who deny the blessing by not acknowledging it, fulfilling its rights, and showing gratitude for it, as mentioned earlier. And Allah knows best.

Al-Qurtubi commented on the other verse: {If you are grateful, I will surely increase you [in favor]} saying that if you thank My blessings upon you, I will increase you from My favor. The verse explicitly states that thankfulness is a cause for increase.

He also explained the verse: {But as for the favor of your Lord, report [it]} as meaning that you should spread what Allah has blessed you with through gratitude and praise. Speaking about Allah's blessings and acknowledging them is thankfulness. The address is to the Prophet, peace be upon him, but the ruling applies to him and others as well. As for the verse {And few of My servants are grateful}, Al-Qurtubi said its meaning is: "Few are those who do this because good is less than evil, and obedience is less than disobedience."

It seems—Allah knows best—that Allah's blessings are numerous and cannot be counted, and they continuously increase upon His servants by His grace. Thankfulness in its various forms requires determination and certainty. Many people fall short and fail to adequately thank and praise the Benefactor. Therefore, the thankful ones are few, and they are the elite. Among these thankfulness leaders is the best of mankind, Muhammad, peace be upon him, because he was the most pious of creation, most knowledgeable of his Creator's rights, and most thankful to Him. This is clearly evident from examining his condition and conduct with his companions, may Allah be pleased with them. This is highlighted in several ways:

1. He used to strive in worship in all its forms, even though he was forgiven for his past and future sins. As narrated by Al-Bukhari and Muslim from the hadith of Al-Mughira bin Shu'ba and Aisha, may Allah be pleased with them, the Prophet used to stand in prayer at night until his feet would crack. Aisha said, "Why do you do this,

O Messenger of Allah, when Allah has forgiven your past and future sins?" He said, "Should I not be a thankful servant?" This is the wording of Aisha's hadith in Al-Bukhari, and both narrations are similar.

2. It was his practice and that of his companions to prostrate in thankfulness when a blessing was renewed or a calamity was averted. As reported by Abu Dawood, At-Tirmidhi, Ibn Majah, and Ahmad from the hadith of Abu Bakra, may Allah be pleased with him, the Prophet would prostrate in thankfulness to Allah when something that pleased him happened or a calamity was removed. Ibn Majah's wording is this, and the others are similar.

Most scholars agreed on the practice of prostrating in thankfulness. Abd al-Rahman bin Ka'ab bin Malik narrated from his father that when Allah accepted his repentance, he prostrated.

3. His guidance to his companions and his statements about thankfulness and explaining its virtue. The Prophet said to someone he saw in tattered clothes, "Do you have wealth?" He replied, "Yes." The Prophet asked, "From what type of wealth?" He said, "Allah has given me camels, sheep, horses, and slaves." The Prophet said, "When Allah gives you wealth, let the effect of Allah's blessing and honor be apparent on you." Abu Dawood, An-Nasa'i, and Al-Hakim narrated this; the wording is from Abu Dawood and Al-Hakim, although Al-Hakim's version is more detailed. An-Nasa'i's wording is similar to Abu Dawood's. Al-Hakim said: The chain is authentic, and neither he nor An-Nasa'i included it. Al-Dhahabi agreed with him, and Al-Albani also authenticated it.

In At-Tirmidhi's narration, from the hadith of Amr bin Shu'aib from his father and grandfather, it is reported: "Indeed, Allah loves to see the effect of His blessing on His servant." At-Tirmidhi said: The hadith is good. He then mentioned similar reports from Abu Al-Ahwas, his father, and Imran bin Husayn and Ibn Mas'ud.

And Al-Albani also authenticated it.

The Prophet, peace be upon him, said: "Whoever says in the morning: 'O Allah, whatever blessing I have this morning is from You alone, with no partner, to You be praise and to You be thanks,' has fulfilled the gratitude for his day. And whoever says the same in the evening has fulfilled the gratitude for his night."

In a hadith reported by Anas, may Allah be pleased with him, in Ibn Majah, the Prophet, peace be upon him, said: "Allah has never bestowed a blessing upon a servant and he says: 'Praise be to Allah,' except that what He has given is better than what He has taken." This means that the praise and gratitude performed is better than the blessing received.

Repentance and Seeking Forgiveness

Repentance is returning to Allah by committing to perform what is required and abandoning what is disliked. It is returning from what Allah dislikes both outwardly and inwardly to what He loves both outwardly and inwardly.

Seeking forgiveness is the act of erasing sin, removing its effects, protecting oneself from its harm, and covering it up. Seeking forgiveness encompasses repentance, and repentance includes seeking forgiveness; each term implies the other when mentioned alone. However, when they are paired, as in the verse: {And ask forgiveness of your Lord and then repent to Him. He will let you enjoy a good provision for a specified term and give every possessor of grace an increase in grace}, seeking forgiveness here is a request for protection from the harm of past actions, and repentance is a return and request for protection from the feared evil of future sins.

It is important to understand that repentance and seeking forgiveness are acts of worship that Allah has commanded us to perform continuously and consistently, whether or not sins or transgressions occur. However, when they do occur—often, as humans are prone to error—it is essential to hasten to repentance, regret, and seek forgiveness abundantly. This worship has immense importance, and it is difficult to fully enumerate its virtues and benefits here. Undoubtedly, it includes Allah's pleasure, proximity to Him, distance from the devil, bringing about good, obtaining blessings, and warding off evils and disliked things. The Quranic texts and prophetic traditions are replete with this, such as Hud's words to his people: {And O my people, ask forgiveness of your Lord and then repent to Him. He will send rain from the sky upon you in showers and increase you in strength added to your strength. And do not turn away, criminals}.

Al-Qurtubi mentioned that seeking forgiveness brings down provisions and rain, and that 'Aad were people of gardens, crops, and construction. When the rain was withheld from them, Hud told them that if they believed and increased their seeking forgiveness, Allah would revive their land and provide them with wealth and children, increasing their strength.

Allah said: {Say, 'Ask forgiveness of your Lord. Indeed, He is ever Forgiving. He will send rain from the sky upon you in showers and give you increase in wealth and children and make gardens for you and make rivers for you}.

It is clear from these verses that repentance, obedience, and abundant seeking forgiveness are causes for the expansion of provisions, the acquisition of wealth, and blessings in it. Thus, Noah, peace be upon him, guided his people to obedience and abundant seeking forgiveness, meaning that if you repent to Allah and seek His forgiveness and obey Him, your provisions will increase, you will be blessed with rain from the sky, and you will benefit from the blessings of the earth, including fertile crops, milk-producing livestock, wealth, and children. He will grant you gardens with various fruits and rivers flowing through them.

Ibn Kathir said: "It is recommended to recite this surah in the prayer for rain because of this verse: {Say, 'Ask forgiveness of your Lord. Indeed, He is ever Forgiving'}." Al-Shabi said: Umar, may Allah be pleased with him, went out to seek rain and did not do anything but seek forgiveness until he returned and rain fell. They said: "We did not see you ask for rain." He said: "I requested rain through the means of the sky that brings down rain." Then he recited: {Ask forgiveness of your Lord. Indeed, He is ever Forgiving}. This was reported by Abdul Razzaq.

The Prophet, peace be upon him, clarified the master of seeking forgiveness as mentioned in Bukhari. He said: "The master of seeking forgiveness is to say: O Allah, You are my Lord, there is no deity but You. You created me, and I am on Your covenant and promise as much as I can. I seek refuge in You from the evil of what I have done. I acknowledge Your blessings upon me, and I acknowledge my sin. So forgive me, for none forgives sins except You..."

It is mentioned in Bukhari that the Prophet, peace be upon him, said: "By Allah, I seek forgiveness from Allah and repent to Him more than seventy times a day." And in Muslim, he said: "I seek forgiveness from Allah a hundred times a day." In another narration: "O people, repent to Allah, for I repent to Him a hundred times a day." All this while the Prophet, peace be upon him, had been forgiven for all his past and future sins, as mentioned in the verse: {Indeed, We have given you a clear victory, That Allah may forgive you what preceded of your sin and what will follow}.

Due to gratitude he, peace be upon him, used to stand in prayer until his feet would crack. When asked, he said: "Should I not be a thankful servant?"

It is clear from the above that repentance and seeking forgiveness are causes for all worldly and otherworldly good.

Among these is the attainment of good and blessings in wealth and the prevention of all harm and disliked things.

Narrated by Abu Dawood, Ibn Majah, An-Nasa'i, Ahmad, At-Tabarani, Al-Hakim, and Al-Bayhaqi from the hadith of Ibn Abbas, may Allah be pleased with them, that the Messenger of Allah, peace be upon him, said: "Whoever persists in seeking forgiveness—according to another wording (more)—Allah will provide a way out for him from every distress, a relief from every anxiety, and will grant him provision from where he does not expect."

Al-Rabi' bin Subayh narrated that a man came to Al-Hasan and complained to him about drought, and Al-Hasan said to him: "Seek forgiveness from Allah." Another man came and complained to him about poverty, and he said: "Seek forgiveness from Allah." Another came and complained to him about the dryness of his gardens, and he said: "Seek forgiveness from Allah." Another came and asked him to pray for a son, and he said: "Seek forgiveness from Allah." We said to him: "You received men complaining to you about various issues, and you instructed all of them to seek forgiveness." He said: "I did not say this from myself, but rather I considered the saying of Allah as reported from His Prophet Noah, peace be upon him, to his people: {Say, 'Ask forgiveness of your Lord. Indeed, He is ever Forgiving. He will send rain from the sky upon you in showers, and give you increase in wealth and children, and make gardens for you and make rivers for you}."

Al-Hafiz Ibn Hajar mentioned this narration from Al-Hasan Al-Basri with some variation in wording, and then said: "It seems that the compiler—meaning Bukhari—hinted at mentioning this verse in reference to Al-Hasan Al-Basri's narration."

Striving for livelihood is taking the necessary means.

Allah, the Almighty, has allocated sustenance according to His knowledge, giving to whom He wills with His wisdom and withholding from whom He wills with His justice. He made some people subservient to others. Allah says: "We have distributed among them their livelihood in the worldly life, and raised some of them above others in degrees that some of them may take others in service. And the mercy of your Lord is better than what they accumulate." [Qur'an, Surah Az-Zukhruf: 32]

Since the matter of wealth is significant and the questioning about it is severe, as the Prophet (peace be upon him) said: "The feet of a servant will not move on the Day of Judgment until he is asked about four things: about his life and how he spent it, about his youth and how he used it, about his wealth from where he earned it and in what he spent it, and about his deeds and what he did with them."

Allah, the Almighty, has commanded His servants to earn a livelihood to help them in His obedience. He says: "And seek the bounty of Allah, and remember Allah much that you may be successful." [Surah Al-Jumua: 10]. Thus, He has made earning a means for worship.

He also says about humans and their love for wealth: "And indeed, he is in the love of wealth intense." [Surah Al-Adiyat: 8].

And He, the Almighty, commands His servants after the completion of a great obligation, which is the Friday prayer: "Then disperse throughout the land and seek from the bounty of Allah." [Surah Al-Jumua: 10].

Imam Al-Baghawi said: This means that when the prayer is completed, disperse in the land for trade and managing your needs.

And when Arak bin Malik (may Allah be pleased with him) finished the Friday prayer, he would stand at the mosque's door and say: "O Allah, I have answered Your call and performed Your obligation, and I have dispersed as You commanded me, so provide me from Your bounty, and You are the best of providers."

Islam has encouraged work and earning, for it is a religion of action, movement, and striving in the land and its cultivation.

The Prophet (peace be upon him) said: "It is better for any of you to take his rope and gather firewood on his back than to go to a man who has been given some of Allah's bounty and ask him, whether he gives or withholds."

And the Prophet (peace be upon him) praised good wealth in the hands of a righteous servant, saying: "What an excellent thing is good wealth in the hands of a righteous man."

The world is not condemned in itself, but rather for the sins, wrongdoings, and consumption of unlawful wealth that occur within it. The forbidden world is that which diverts one from religion and is accumulated from the forbidden. That is, it is gathered from the forbidden and used in the forbidden.

The Prophet (peace be upon him) said: "The world is for four types of people: A man who gathers wealth from lawful sources and spends it in what is right, this one is in the highest of ranks.

And a man who gathers wealth from unlawful sources and spends it in what is right, this one is in the worst of ranks.

And a man who gathers wealth from unlawful sources and spends it in unlawful ways, this one is in the worst of ranks.

And a man who gathers wealth from lawful sources and spends it in unlawful ways, this one is in the worst of ranks."

Work is obligatory, and earning is a duty for those who have dependents or responsibilities. Islam has deemed neglecting the rights of one's spouse unacceptable.

Work is obligatory and earning a livelihood is a duty for those who have dependents or responsibilities. Islam has deemed neglecting the rights of one's spouse, children, and parents as grave sins. For example, Wahb ibn Jaber reported: "I witnessed Abdullah ibn Amr ibn al-As in Jerusalem. A freedman of his came to him and said: 'I intend to stay here for this month'—meaning Ramadan. Abdullah asked: 'Have you left for your family what will sustain them?' He said: 'No.' Abdullah said: 'If not, then return and leave them what will sustain them. I heard the Messenger of Allah (peace be upon him) say: 'It is enough sin for a person to neglect those whom he is responsible for providing sustenance.'"

And Ibn Abbas (may Allah be pleased with them) said: "When the Messenger of Allah (peace be upon him) saw a man and admired him, he would ask: 'Does he have a profession?' If they said no, he would lose interest in him. It was asked: 'Why is that, O Messenger of Allah?' He said: 'Because if a believer does not have a profession, he lives by his religion.'"

A Muslim is rewarded for providing for his family, as the Prophet (peace be upon him) said: "A dinar you spend in the cause of Allah, a dinar you spend to free a slave, a dinar you give in charity to a poor person, and a dinar you spend on your family, the greatest reward is for the dinar you spend on your family."

It is narrated that Sufyan al-Thawri (may Allah have mercy on him) said: "You should engage in the work of champions. Earning from lawful sources and spending on your dependents."

And when someone came to him seeking knowledge, he would ask whether they had a means of livelihood. If they were financially secure, he would advise them to seek knowledge, but if not, he would advise them to seek a livelihood.

Ayyub al-Sakhtiyani said: Abu Qilabah said to me: "O Ayyub, stick to your market, for it provides independence from people and righteousness in religion."

Muhammad ibn Sirin reported from his father: "I prayed with Umar ibn al-Khattab the Maghrib prayer. Afterward, a group of Quraysh left with him and saw a bundle under his armpit. He asked: 'What is this, O ibn Sirin?' I said: 'O Commander of the Faithful, I come to the market to buy and sell.' Umar then said to the Quraysh: 'Do not let this and similar things in trade overpower you, for trade is one-third of governance.'"

Abu Sulayman al-Darani said: "Worship is not about sitting idle while others provide for you. Rather, begin by earning your own bread and then worship."

Wealth in the hands of a Muslim is a means to a dignified life in this world and happiness in the hereafter. As Said ibn al-Musayyib said: "There is no good in someone who does not want to earn lawful wealth, give its due rights, and keep himself from needing others."

Ibn Qudamah detailed the situation of those seeking worldly gains: "We have clarified that wealth is not condemned in itself; rather, it should be praised because it is a means to achieve religious and worldly benefits. Allah called it good and it sustains human life. Allah says at the beginning of Surah An-Nisa: 'And do not give your property, which

Allah has made a means of support for you, to the foolish.' (An-Nisa: 5)."

Abu Ishaq al-Sabi'i said: "They considered prosperity as an aid to religion."

Sufyan said: "In our time, wealth is the weapon of the believers."

In summary: Wealth is like a snake that contains both poison and an antidote. Its antidote is its benefits, and its poison is its dangers. Those who understand its benefits can protect themselves from its harm and obtain its good.

Wealth is not condemned in itself; rather, condemnation occurs due to the nature of human behavior, whether due to excessive greed, acquiring it unlawfully, withholding it from its rightful place, spending it in the wrong ways, or showing off with it. Allah says: "Indeed, your wealth and your children are but a trial." (At-Taghabun: 15).

In the Sunan of Tirmidhi, the Prophet (peace be upon him) said: "Two hungry wolves sent into a flock of sheep do not cause more corruption than a person's greed for wealth and honor does to his religion."

The predecessors were fearful of the trial of wealth. Yahya ibn Mu'adh said: "The dirham is a scorpion. If you do not know how to treat it, do not take it, for if it stings you, its poison will kill you." He was asked: "What is its treatment?" He said: "Taking it from its lawful source and using it for its rightful purpose."

He also said about the owner of wealth: "There are two calamities for a person in his wealth at his death, which no one else hears of: it is taken from him entirely, and he is questioned about it entirely."

The religion of Islam is the religion of trust, not negligence, and the religion of striving, not idleness.

Umar (may Allah be pleased with him) said: "None of you should sit idly asking Allah to provide for you; you know that the sky does not rain gold or silver."

Muhammad ibn al-Munkadir said in beautiful words about wealth: "Wealth is a great aid to piety."

Contentment is not to seek an alternative ... it contains comfort and ease of body. Look at those who owned the whole world - Did they leave it without more than a shroud and coffin? (1)

My dear friend:

Know that asceticism is not in abandoning wealth, but in using it generously and with strength to win hearts. True asceticism is to abandon the world for the sake of knowledge, recognizing its insignificance compared to the preciousness of the hereafter. Those who understand that the world is like melting snow and the hereafter is like lasting pearls will be more eager to exchange this for that.

The asceticism of the predecessors was due to their fear of falling into forbidden actions. Muzammil said: "I visited Sufyan while he was eating meat with eggs, and I spoke to him about it. He said: 'I did not command you not to eat good things; earn from lawful sources and eat well.'"

Ali ibn al-Fudail said: "I heard my father say to Ibn al-Mubarak: 'You advise us to be ascetic, to live simply, and to have enough, yet you bring goods from Khurasan to the sacred city. How is this?' Ibn al-Mubarak replied: 'O Abu Ali, I do this to preserve my dignity, honor my reputation, and help me in the obedience of my Lord.'"

[Reasons for Sustenance]

The reasons for sustenance are numerous and varied, among the most important of which are: adherence to piety. Allah says: "If only the people of those towns had believed and been conscious of Allah, We would certainly have opened up to them blessings from the heavens and the earth. But they denied, so We seized them for what they used to earn." (Al-A'raf: 96). And He says regarding seeking forgiveness and repentance and their benefits: "Say, 'Ask forgiveness of your Lord. Indeed, He is Forgiving. He will send rain from the sky upon you in continuing showers, and give you increase in wealth and children and make gardens for you and make rivers for you.'" (Nuh: 10-12).

Among the greatest reasons for attracting sustenance is abandoning sins and transgressions, for they deprive one of the goodness of both this world and the Hereafter.

Allah says: "Whatever strikes you of disaster is because of what your own hands have earned, and He pardons much." (Ash-Shura: 30), meaning due to your own wrongdoing.

The Prophet (peace be upon him) said: "A man may be deprived of sustenance due to a sin he commits."

A scholar was asked: "Is it not true that one who fears Allah will have a way out and will be provided for from unexpected sources?" The scholar replied: "By Allah, He certainly provides us with a way out, though we have not reached the level of piety deserving of it, and He certainly provides us with sustenance even though we have not achieved sufficient piety. And we hope for the third benefit: that one who fears Allah will have his sins forgiven and will have his reward increased."

Some of the early Muslims were amazed at how someone who disobeys Allah the Almighty is still provided for by the generous and forbearing

One. They said: "I am astonished at how someone who prays the dawn prayer after the sun has risen is still provided for!"

Where are we compared to them:

The world was not their greatest concern or ultimate goal. It did not distract them. They were aware of Allah's other blessings, the greatest and most important of which was the blessing of Islam, followed by the blessings of health and security in the homeland: "And if you should count the favor of Allah, you could not enumerate it." (Ibrahim: 34).

Hassan ibn Salih said: "Sometimes I would wake up with not a single dirham with me, and it was as if the entire world had been gathered for me."

Their connection to Allah was strong, and their fear of sins was intense. Therefore, they would see the effects of minor sins on their animals, their wives, and their children!

For them, wealth was a means, and the ultimate goal and aspiration was Paradise. Therefore, their concerns and responses were focused on the Hereafter, which was the ultimate objective and the highest place.

Abu Hazim the ascetic was asked about his wealth. He said: "Two things, neither of which makes me fear poverty: trust in Allah and despair of what is in the hands of people."

"Implore Allah, do not implore people, and be content with despair, for honor lies in despair. And be independent of close relatives and family, for true wealth is independence from people."

For those whom Allah has made wealthy and who have been given blessings, let them thank Allah for His blessings, use them in His obedience, and distribute them generously to those with rights and to fulfill needs.

Ibn Taymiyyah said: "He should take wealth with a generous spirit, to be blessed in it, without giving it a place in his heart. Seeking it should be like tending to a latrine."

He continued: "Thus, wealth should be used for one's needs like a donkey one rides, or a mat one sits on, or like a latrine where one relieves oneself without being enslaved by it, instead of becoming impatient when touched by harm and withholding when touched by good."

Allah's sustenance is written and predetermined. It is neither brought by the eagerness of the eager nor repelled by the laziness of the lazy. Allah the Almighty has allocated sustenance with His knowledge and justice, which is why those who claim: 'I was given it only because of knowledge I have.'" are disbelievers. It is a divine grant to test His servants!

Maryam al-Basri said: "I have not worried about sustenance or exhausted myself in seeking it since I heard Allah the Almighty say: 'And in the heaven is your provision and whatever you are promised.'" (Adh-Dhariyat: 22).

"If a door is closed to you without a need, let it be for another door to open for you. For the contents of your belly are sufficient if filled, and avoiding indecent matters is enough for you."

"Do not be wasteful of your honor and avoid committing sins, as avoiding them will keep you from their misfortunes."

The Prophet (peace be upon him) warned that if the world and its food become a Muslim's greatest concern and habit day and night, distracting them from obedience and worship, he said: "Whoever wakes up with the world as his greatest concern, Allah will place his poverty before his eyes, scatter his affairs, and he will receive only what was decreed for him of the world. But whoever wakes up with the

Hereafter as his greatest concern, Allah will place wealth in his heart, gather his affairs, and the world will come to him willingly. Allah is quicker in bringing about good for him."

Ibn al-Qayyim, may Allah have mercy on him, said: "This is the true poverty and true wealth. If this is wealth for someone whose greatest concern is the Hereafter, how about someone whose greatest concern is Allah the Almighty? This serves as a reminder and is more fitting."

Many verses have been revealed addressing luxury and those who live in luxury, and the negative impact it has on many people. Allah says: "Until, when We seize their affluent ones with punishment, at once they are crying to Allah for help." (Al-Mu'minun: 64) And He says about the people of the left hand: "Indeed, they were, before that, indulging in affluence." (Al-Waqi'ah: 45) He also says: "And when We intend to destroy a city, We command its affluent ones, and they commit corruption therein. And the word becomes obligatory upon it, and We destroy it with complete destruction." (Al-Isra: 16) And in another verse: "And We did not send into any city any warner except its affluent ones said, 'Indeed, we are, in that which you have been sent with, disbelievers.'" (Saba: 34)

Regarding wealth, houses, and palaces, as Shaykh al-Islam Ibn Taymiyyah said about the categorization of people with wealth: "Poverty suits many character traits, while wealth suits only a few. That is why the majority of those who enter Paradise are the poor, for the trial of poverty is lighter. Both poverty and wealth require patience and gratitude, but since pleasure is found in prosperity and pain in adversity, gratitude is commonly mentioned in prosperity and patience in adversity."

Thus, a person's wealth has limited benefit by itself, whether it is food to eat, clothes to wear, or a means of transport. But for those whom Allah wills good, they spend from it, give charity, provide support, and bring relief. This is indeed the best kind of wealth!

The Prophet (peace be upon him) said: "The son of Adam says, 'My wealth!' But is there anything of your wealth except what you have eaten and consumed, what you have worn and worn out, or what you have given in charity and sent ahead?"

Yahya ibn Mu'adh said: "Woe to the son of Adam! If he feared the Fire as he fears poverty, he would enter Paradise."

Because of this fear and apprehension, they would be cautious and hold themselves accountable, desiring salvation and fearing destruction.

Khurami ibn Yunus said: "I heard Abu Yusuf al-Ghuli say: I have been scrutinizing my food for sixty years."

Most people today fit the poet's description:

"We patch up our world by tearing our religion ... So neither our religion remains nor what we patch."

That is why tears have become rare and fear of Allah is less common.

Sahl, may Allah have mercy on him, said: "You will not find true fear until you consume only what is lawful."

Ali ibn Hafs al-Bazzaz said: "Hafs ibn Abdulrahman was a partner of Abu Hanifah, and Abu Hanifah would prepare him. He once sent him merchandise and informed him of a defect in a particular garment, saying: 'If you sell it, make sure to disclose it.' Hafs sold the merchandise and forgot to disclose the defect, not knowing who he sold it to. When Abu Hanifah learned of it, he gave away the entire price of the merchandise as charity."

My dear brother: Where are we compared to these people?

Muslim ibn Abdulmalik said: "I entered upon Umar ibn Abdulaziz after Fajr in a room where he would seclude himself after Fajr, and no one would enter. A maid brought him a dish with dates on it, and he liked dates. He picked up a handful and said: 'O Muslim, do you think if a man ate this and then drank water with it—dates are sweet—would it sustain him until evening?' I said: 'I don't know.' He then picked up more and said: 'What about this?' I said: 'Yes, O Commander of the Faithful, it was enough for him without this, to the extent that he did not care if he did not taste any other food.'

And from Muzzammil: "I heard Wahb ibn al-Ward say: 'If you stand as long as this pillar in worship, it will not benefit you until you ensure that what enters your stomach is lawful and not unlawful.'"

When Hudhayfah al-Marashi saw people rushing to the first row in prayer, he said: "They should rush to eating lawful bread, not to the first row."

Satan is in conflict and striving to mislead the Muslim and prevent him from the path of Allah.

Yusuf ibn Asbat said: "When a young man worships, Satan says: 'Look at where his food comes from.' If his food is from a source of wrongdoing, he says: 'Leave him, do not occupy yourselves with him; let him strive and toil, for he has received his share.'"

Allah the Almighty may make the blessing of wealth a means of gradual punishment for those who disobey Him and go against His commands, as we have heard about previous nations and seen in contemporary nations and states. Allah says: "And Allah sets forth an example of a city that was secure and at ease, its provision coming to it in abundance from every place, but it denied the favors of Allah. So Allah made it taste the clothing of hunger and fear for what they had been doing." (An-Nahl: 112)

Shu'ayb ibn Harb said: "Do not underestimate a small coin with which you obey Allah in earning it. It is not the coin that is desired, but the obedience. Perhaps you will buy some vegetables with it, and it will not settle in your stomach before you are forgiven."

"I see garments preserved for people ... And morals that are trampled and not preserved."

"They say the time is corrupt ... Yet they are corrupt, and the time is not."

Some of the predecessors said: "To leave a dinar from what Allah dislikes is more beloved to me than five hundred pilgrimages."

That is why Al-Hasan said: "I saw seventy of those who participated in Badr being more ascetic in what Allah has made lawful for them than you are in what Allah has forbidden."

"Money goes away, whether lawful or unlawful ... And it remains in the future with its sins."

"The pious one is not pious to his God ... Until his drink and food are pure ... And what he possesses is pure and his hand pours it ... And his speech is good and truthful."

As for truthful speech in buying and selling, you see remarkable conditions among those!

And Maimun ibn Mehran said: "A man is not pious until he holds himself to account more strictly than a partner does to his partner, and until he knows where his clothing, food, and drink come from."

The righteous wife and daughter assist in ensuring lawful earnings and pleasant food.

The daughter of Al-'Adawiyya said to her father: "O my father, I will not excuse you from consuming what is unlawful." He replied: "What if I can only find unlawful food?" She said: "We will endure hunger in this world rather than endure the Fire in the Hereafter."

And Al-Mu'afa ibn Imran said: "There were ten among those who preceded us in knowledge who were very meticulous about what was lawful. They would not consume anything except what they knew was lawful. Otherwise, they would eat dirt. Among them were Bishr, Ibrahim ibn Adham, Sulaiman al-Khawwas, Ali ibn al-Fudayl, Abu Ma'awiya al-Aswad, Yusuf ibn Asbat, Wahb ibn al-Ward, Hudhayfa, a Sheikh from Harran, and Dawud al-Tayi."

Bishr used to say: "A man should consider where his bread comes from and the origin of the place he lives in, then he should speak."

Ali ibn Shu'ayb said: "My father said to me: 'I was once with such-and-such person,' and he said: 'Did you eat with him?' I said: 'Yes.' He said: 'Praise Allah. You ate what you will not be questioned about, meaning regarding its earnings.'"

And Abu Yusuf al-Ghassuli said: "Twelve dirhams are sufficient for me for a year, one dirham each month. Nothing drives me to work except the tongues of these scholars, who say: 'Where does Abu Yusuf eat from?'"

He used to say: "I have been learning the law of my food for sixty years."

And Khalaf ibn Tamim asked Ibrahim ibn Adham: "Since when have you come to Sham?" He replied: "For twenty-four years. I did not come for military service or jihad. I came to satisfy myself with lawful bread."

And Ibn Mubarak said: "To reject a dirham from a doubt is more beloved to me than to give charity of one hundred thousand dirhams, and one hundred thousand, until it reached six hundred thousand."

Consider this jurisprudential question: It is not about the answer ... but the question itself is a precaution and a discharge of liability!

Imam Ahmad was asked about a man who had three dirhams, one of which he did not recognize. He, may Allah have mercy on him, said: "He should not eat from it until he recognizes it."

They used to advise each other to be diligent in seeking even a small amount of lawful earnings, as it contains sufficiency and blessing.

Bishr ibn al-Harith said: "A man should not be satisfied with lawful earnings today, because when he is satisfied with the lawful, his soul will urge him toward the unlawful. So, how about these amounts today?"

"Whoever praises the world for the ease of his living ... will surely, in truth, reproach it for a little.

When it turns away, it is a regret for the person ... and when it comes, it brings many worries."

O Muslim brother,

Amr ibn Qais al-Mala'i, when he looked at the people of the marketplace, would say: "How heedless these people are of what is prepared for them!"

My beloved brother:

A person desires to be given what he wishes ... and God wills only what He desires.

The person says: "My benefit and my wealth" ... and piety to God is the best thing they have gained.

May God have mercy on the noble companion Abu al-Darda, who said: "Part of a man's understanding is to improve his livelihood."

He, may God be pleased with him, said: "The rectification of livelihood is from the rectification of religion, and the rectification of religion is from the rectification of the mind."

Umar ibn al-Khattab, may God be pleased with him, addressing the reciters, said: "O assembly of reciters, compete in doing good deeds, seek from the grace of God, and do not become dependent on others."

It is narrated about Mubarak Abu Abdullah: He used to work in a garden for his master, and he stayed there for a long time. One day, his master, who was one of the merchants of Hamadan, came to him and said: "O Mubarak, I want sweet pomegranates."

So Mubarak went to some trees and brought pomegranates from them. When his master cracked them open, he found them sour and became angry with him, saying: "You sought sweetness and brought me sour ones! Bring me sweet ones."

Mubarak went and picked from another tree. When his master cracked them open, they were also sour, and his anger intensified. He did this a third time, and they were also sour. Then his master asked him:

"Do you not know the difference between sweet and sour?"

He replied: "No."

His master asked: "Why is that?" He said: "Because I have not eaten any of it to know."

His master asked: "And why did you not eat it?"

He said: "Because you did not permit me to eat from it."

The owner of the garden was astonished by this, and when he realized the sincerity of his servant, he esteemed him greatly and increased his honor. He had a daughter who had been proposed to many times. He asked Mubarak: "Who do you think should marry this daughter?"

He replied: "The people of ignorance married for lineage, the Jews for wealth, and the Christians for beauty. But this nation marries for religion."

The man was pleased with his wisdom and went to tell his wife. He said: "I do not see a better match for this daughter than Mubarak."

He married her off to him and gave them a large amount of money. They had Abdullah ibn al-Mubarak, the scholar, the hadith scholar, the ascetic, and the warrior, who was the noblest fruit of marriage in his time. Even Fudayl ibn Iyad, may God have mercy on him, swore by his statement: "By the Lord of this house, my eyes have not seen anyone like ibn al-Mubarak."

Today, with the widespread deceit and fraud in the lives of some people, it is rare to find someone who is truthful and trustworthy in fulfilling their trust, and who stays away from deceit and trickery!

And while the outcome of sin is clear and known in the Hereafter, its consequence in this world is closer!

It is mentioned that Umar ibn al-Khattab, may God be pleased with him, prohibited the mixing of milk with water during his caliphate. One night, he went out on the outskirts of the city and heard a woman say to her daughter: "Mix the milk with water."

The daughter said: "How can I mix it when the Commander of the Faithful has prohibited mixing?"

The mother said: "The people have mixed it, so mix it; what does the Commander of the Faithful know?"

The daughter replied: "If Umar does not know, then the God of Umar knows. I would not do it since he has prohibited it."

Umar was impressed by her words. He called his son Asim and said:

"My son, go to such and such place and inquire about the girl - describing her to him."

Asim went and found that she was a girl from Banu Hilal. Umar said to him:

"Go, my son, and marry her. She is likely to bring forth a leader who will lead the Arabs."

Asim ibn Omar married her, and she gave birth to Umm Asim, the daughter of Asim ibn Omar ibn al-Khattab. She married Abdulaziz ibn Marwan ibn al-Hakam, and she gave birth to Umar ibn Abdulaziz.

As for the effect of unlawful money, it is clear, even if the money is small and the man is a warrior. Umar ibn al-Khattab, may God be pleased with him, said: "When it was the day of Khaybar, a group of the Prophet's companions came and said: 'So-and-so is a martyr, and so-and-so is a martyr,' until they passed by a man and said: 'So-and-so is a martyr.' The Prophet, peace be upon him, said: 'No, he is in the Fire wearing a cloak he took unjustly - or a garment.'"

Where are we compared to these people?

Bishr ibn al-Mufaddal said: "A woman came with a brocade to Yunus ibn Ubaid, offering it to him. He asked her: 'How much?' She said: 'Sixty dirhams.' He gave it to his neighbor and said: 'How do you see it?' He said: 'Twenty and a hundred.' Bishr said: 'I see that as its price, or close to its price.' He said to her: 'Go and consult your family about selling it for twenty-five and a hundred.' She said: 'They instructed me to sell it for sixty.' He said: 'Return and consult them again.'"

A shipment of goods was brought to Imam Bukhari, sent by Abu Hafs, one of his father's close students. Some merchants came to him offering to buy the goods with a profit of five thousand dirhams.

He told them: "Leave tonight." The next day, other merchants came and offered a profit of ten thousand dirhams for the goods. He turned them away and said: "I intended last night to give it to the first group, so I gave it to them and said: 'I do not wish to go back on my intention.'"

There are many doors to sustenance, but its widest door and strongest cause is the fear of God, frequent charity, prayer, and seeking forgiveness. As God Almighty says: "And whoever fears Allah—He will make for him a way out And will provide for him from where he does not expect" [Quran 65:2-3]. And He says: "And if the people of those towns had believed and been God-fearing, We would certainly have opened up to them blessings from the heavens and the earth" [Quran 7:96]. And He says: "And whatever you spend of anything—He will replace it. And He is the best of providers" [Quran 34:39].

The Prophet, peace be upon him, said: "Whoever persists in seeking forgiveness, Allah will make for him a way out from every distress, and a relief from every hardship, and will provide for him from where he does not expect." Narrated by Ahmad, Abu Dawood, and Al-Hakim, who said: "It has a sound chain of narrators."

Among the causes of deprivation is sins and transgressions; it has been narrated by Al-Hakim in his Mustadrak—though its chain of narrators has been questioned—that the Prophet, peace be upon him, said: "Indeed, supplication can avert decree, and righteousness increases sustenance, and indeed a servant may be deprived of sustenance due to the sins he commits."

B: Professor Doctor Fazal Elahi's Appeal

On this occasion, I strongly appeal to all Muslims around the world to adopt the means of earning sustenance as mentioned in the Quran and Sunnah as their safeguard. All types of goodness, prosperity, and happiness are found in following the path prescribed by Allah, the Owner of the Kingdom. He Himself says:

{O you who have believed, respond to Allah and to the Messenger when he calls you to that which gives you life. And know that Allah intervenes between a man and his heart and that to Him you will be gathered.}

And all forms of evil, distress, and misfortune are due to deviating from the path of Allah. He Himself said:

{And whoever turns away from My remembrance – indeed, he will have a depressed life, and We will gather him on the Day of Resurrection blind. He will say, 'My Lord, why have You raised me blind while I was [once] seeing?' Allah will say, 'Thus did Our signs come to you, and you forgot them; and thus will you this Day be forgotten.'}

May Allah grant us all the ability to follow His path. Amen, O Ever-Living, O Sustainer. And may Allah's blessings and peace be upon our Prophet, his family, his companions, and his followers. And our final supplication is, "Praise be to Allah, Lord of the worlds."

Bibliography:

1. Rizq ki Kunjiyaan by Professor Doctor Fazal Elahi

2. Kitaab ar-Rizq Abwaabuhu wa MafaatiHuhu by [Abdul Malik bin Qasim

3. al-Barakah fi ar-Rizq wal-Asbaab al-Jaalibah Laha fi Daw' al-Kitaab wal-Sunnah by Abdullah as-Suwalmah